The
Heart Felt
Letters

'A Tragedy Aired is a
Tragedy Shared'

The
Heart Felt
Letters

'A Tragedy Aired is a
Tragedy Shared'

By

MAINSTREAM
PUBLISHING

EDINBURGH AND LONDON

First published in Great Britain in 1998 by
MAINSTREAM PUBLISHING COMPANY (EDINBURGH) LTD
7 Albany Street
Edinburgh EH1 3UG

ISBN 1 84018 128 1

Acknowledgements are due to the following people for their kind permission to use their
pictures in this publication: Virgin Radio for the picture of Richard Branson and Chris
Evans; Star Images for the picture of Lord and Lady Lloyd-Webber; and *The Sun* for the
picture of Robin and Gaynor Cook

A catalogue record for this book is available from the British Library

Printed and bound in Great Britain by Butler and Tanner Ltd, Frome

Heart Felt Productions Limited

'A Tragedy Aired is a Tragedy Shared'

Dawn Airey
Channel 5 Television
22 Long Acre
London WC2

Suites 139/40
Elm Park Mansions
Park Walk
LONDON
SW10 0AS
Tel: 0171-353-9689
Fax: 0171-376-8378

17th July 1997

Dear Dawn,

Hi there! Listen - we've literally been commissioned by the BBC to do an <u>Omnibus</u> on 'dumbing down' (awful expression!) in the media.Yeah - <u>that</u> old one!

The take is to assemble a panel of celebs prepared to defend 'lowest common denominator product'. First (natch!) we rang Jane Root - she's Head of Independent Commissions at the BBC, Dawn - but she suggested you.Then we ran into a slight problem. Our producer at the BBC wanted Mark Lawson to chair the show.

"Not in this life, pal!" I said.

I mean, has he swallowed the dictionary or what? Now it's between Joanna Lumley, Griff Rhys-Jones and Karen Krizanovitch.Do you know Karen, Dawn? She's the bums and boobs correspondent of the new, in ya face, Independent, and is <u>she</u> a mega-babe!

Blonde, 5ft 8ins, great legs, tits to die for, bagsa attitude.

Hey - how much do you hate this gal!
Have a great one! (Oh - recording date, end of October.)

"Cuuuuuue Kirsty!"
Yours,

Liz

Liz Reed.

Directors: Jeff Boyd Liz Reed Martin Jacques
Simon King, Angela Picano (Sicily)
Registered in England NO: 2905691

Dawn Airey
Director of Programmes

24 July 1997

Liz Reed
Heart Felt Productions Limited
Suites 139/140
Elm Park Mansions
Park Walk
London SW10 0AS

Dear Liz

OMNIBUS

Thanks for your letter of 17 July, and apologies for the slight delay in responding but life is more than hectic, trying to run a new Channel.
I am afraid the diary is so choc-a-bloc at present, I just cannot commit the time this would need. In addition, I am hoping to go off on holiday at the end of August/beginning of September which would make the October deadline impossible.

I am sorry I cannot take part, but wish you well with the project.
With best wishes

Yours

Dawn Airey

Channel 5 Broadcasting Limited 22 Long Acre London WC23 9LY
Telephone : 0171 550 5555 Facsimile: 0171 550 5554

Registered in England no: 3147460

Heart Felt Productions Limited

'A Tragedy Aired is a Tragedy Shared'

Michael Jackson
Channel Four Television
124 Horseferry Road
London SW1

17th July 1997

Suites 139/140
Elm Park Mansions
Park Walk
LONDON
SW10 0AS
Tel: 0171-352-9689
Fax: 0171-376-8378

Dear Michael

'ARE DOCTORS PLAYING GOD, OR GIVING WORKING MUMS A LIFE-LINE?'

Good question. Or is it? Maybe it's just another way of saying that Channel 4 has been short of TOT (Triumph over Tragedy) product.

Here's the pitch: what we call a 'High Concept' show, Michael - a TV programme, which, like, evokes the whole, you know, syndrome of modern empirical experience.

I'm talking tabloid values transferred to TV - mothers, sex fiends, dealers in death, mega-babes with great bazongas. Plus I'm talking the wacky side of tragedy, tragedy with production values.

Tragedy can be sexy, yeah?

Not moral panic. That was very 1996. Ambitious crusading women at No 10? Who needs 'em!
To a distraught mother or the legless victim of an outrage, the Heart Felt team would be first up with an offer. "OK, so you're grieving now, but that's good, that's healing - but hold on to the positive aspects of catastrophe. A Christmas single . . . Robson and Jerome . . . Bob Hoskins . . . Richard Branson grinning in the wings . . . sign here."

Bosh. Sorted.

What's your take on this one, Michael? We'd appreciate your input. What about presenters? (Not Jeremy Isaacs.)

Possible titles: 'MOTHERS AGAINST MURDER!' 'WHO PUT HEROIN IN MY KIDDIES' SWEETS?' Which do you prefer?

Hey - let's make a difference!
Yours

Jeff Boyd

Directors: Jeff Boyd Liz Reed Martin Jacques
Simon King, Angela Picano (Sicily)
Registered in England NO: 2905691

Heart Felt Productions Limited

'A Tragedy Aired is a Tragedy Shared'

Jane Root
Independent Commissions
The BBC
Television Centre
London W12.

Suites 139/140
Elm Park Mansions
Park Walk
LONDON SW10 0AS

23rd July 1997

Dear Jane

'WHO PUT HEROIN IN MY KIDDIES' SWEETS?'

That's the title, Jane - and here's the format: a five nights-a-week, one-hour-programme structured like a tabloid. Thus:

Page 1. A catastrophe. An upturned hovercraft in Dover Harbour. Floating old folk clutching duty-free bags. If there hasn't been a catastrophe we settle for a scandal. Lebanese valve victims on their way to Harley Street with poor people's organs in an ice-bucket.

Page 2. 'YOU THE JURY!' Myra Hindley. Should she:
(a) Rot in gaol?
(b) Be let loose to murder your innocent children? You decide!

Page 3. 'CRUMPET COUNTDOWN!' The best of British, chosen by the totty watchers of FHM magazine. Babes with great bazongas.

Page 4. 'HARD NEWS!' 'Call off the Wedding! The Bride's in a Coma!' 'I Bonked Posh Spice when she was Sweet Sixteen!' 'A Fiend on the Loose in Hay-On-Wye.' Whichever does it for us on the day.

Page 5. 'PULL THE OTHER ONE!' A think-piece to camera by the 'Man whose Bite is Worse than his Bark!' Lord Tebbit. Keith Waterhouse. Judge Pickles. TV Anne Robinson. Richard Littlejohn.

Page 6. 'LET'S GET SOMEONE INTO TROUBLE!' Shop your friends and family down the Heart Felt Grass-Up Line! 'My son the dole cheat!' 'My crippled mother smokes cannabis!'

Plus the latest goss on pop and sport.

Hey - does that blow your skirt up, Jane? I certainly hope so!

Have a great one!

Yours

Liz

Liz Reed.

Directors: Jeff Boyd Liz Reed Martin Jacques
Simon King, Angela Picano (Sicily)
Registered in England NO: 2905691

CHANNEL FOUR TELEVISION   124 HORSEFERRY ROAD,LONDON SWIP 2TX
TELEPHONE: 0171-396-4444. DIRECT LINE: 0171-306 8700
FAX: 0171-306 8356.
MINICOM: 0171-306 8691
EMAIL: CLANGDON@CHANNEL4.CO.UK
MICHAEL JACKSON CHIEF EXECUTIVE

Jeff Boyd
Heart Felt Productions Ltd
Suites 139/140
Elm Park Mansions
Park Walk
London
SW10 0AS

21 July 1997

Dear Jeff

Thank you for your letter of July 17.

Unfortunately, although I've given your idea serious consideration,
I'm unable to pursue it.

I'm sorry to disappoint you. As you can imagine, we receive an
enormous number of proposals each year and only a few of them are
able to go into production.

Thanks again for writing.

Best wishes,

Michael Jackson

CHANNEL FOUR TELEVISION
SIR MICHAEL BISHOP CBE(CHAIRMAN), DAVID PLOWRIGHT(DEPUTY CHAIRMAN)
MICHAEL JACKSON(CHIEF EXECUTIVE), STEWART BUTTERFIELD (DIRECTOR ADVERTISING SALES AND MARKETING), COLIN LEVENTHAL (DIRECTOR
OF ACQUISITION),
FRANK McGETTIGAN (DIRECTOR AND GENERAL MANAGER), DAVID SCOTT (MANAGING DIRECTOR), JOHN WILLIS(DIRECTOR OF PROGRAMMES),
SECRETARY: ANDREW YEATES

Heart Felt Productions Limited

'A Tragedy Aired is a Tragedy Shared'

James Boyle   Suites 139/140
Radio 4   Elm Park Mansions
Broadcasting House   Park Walk
LONDON W1.   LONDON
                               SW10 0AS
25th July 1997   Tel: 0171-352-9689
                               Fax: 0171-376-8378

Dear James,
Hi there! Hey — we met aeons ago in Jeremy Gibson's
office in Bristol. I hope you remember. I certainly do!

So — your parameters as per Birtism (ouch!) are to dumb
down Radio 4. Well, how about replacing Ned Sherrin on
'Loose Ends' either with Vic and Bob or with Lee Hurst?
Ned's cool, but that bit he does, you know, his schtick,
it's what, it's satire, right? But satire's a very
Sixties syndrome, and the Sixties are kinda late
Eighties, early Nineties yeah?

But Vic and Bob are literally bananas. Sample bit:
"What's that you're eating, Vic? A piece of chocolate?"
"No, Bob. It's dog-shit."

Surreal or what? For me it's between Vic and Bob and Lee
Hurst.

Sample bit by Lee Hurst:
"Hey — why are you sitting down, Lee?"
"I'm having a crap."

Off the wall or what?
And here's a possible pilot. 'WITH FRIENDS LIKE THIS . .
. . . .' In the studio hot-seat, a celeb who, in spite of
mega achievements, is thought by everyone to be a total
pillock. Jeffrey Archer. Andrew Lloyd-Webber. Janet
Street-Porter. Jeremy Isaacs. Whoever.

His friends line up to speak on his behalf. But then
things go horribly wrong!
Or maybe something with Sue Gaisford?

Does one of these tighten your nuts, James? I certainly
hope so.
See ya!
Yours,

Liz

Liz Reed.

Directors: Jeff Boyd Liz Reed Martin Jacques
Simon King, Angela Picano (Sicily)
Registered in England NO: 2905691

BRITISH BROADCASTING CORPORATION
BROADCASTING HOUSE
PORTLAND PLACE
LONDON W1A 1AA
TELEPHONE:0171 580 4468

Liz Reed
Heart Felt Productions Limited,
Suites 139/140,
Elm Park Mansions,
Park Walk
LONDON.
SW10 0AS

1st August 1997

Dear Liz,

Thanks for your letter. Of course I remember meeting you.

I am not 'dumbing-down' Radio 4 – I don't know who made that word up but it hasn't and won't feature in my vocabulary. I am perfectly happy with Ned and 'Loose Ends'.

You may be aware that the commissioning process has changed somewhat in Radio 4 and programme proposals should be sent to my Commissioning Editor in October for a view. In order to retain clarity and fairness in this process I have decided not to review any proposals until they have been sent through the proper process.

If you would like to discuss the commissioning process in detail, I suggest you contact Caroline Elliot who will be taking up the post of Network Manager, Radio 4 in mid-August.
Many thanks for thinking of Radio 4. It was good to hear from you again.

Yours sincerely,

(James Boyle)

Heart Felt Productions Limited

'A Tragedy Aired is a Tragedy Shared'

Richard Branson
Virgin Records
Kensal House
553 Harrow Road
London W8

Suites 139/140
Elm Park Mansions
Park Walk
LONDON
SW10 0\AS

14th August 1997

Tel: 0171-3252-9689
Fax: 0171-376-8378

Dear Richard,

Okay, so it's early days yet, but shouldn't we be priori-
tising plans for a Christmas 'A' side? Basically I'm suggesting that we pool our thinking compassion-wise.

Here at Heart Felt we're kicking ourselves for missing out
on the tenth anniversary of the Hungerford thing - but,
hey, give it up to Lucy Jago and the guys at the Community
Unit for being so quick out of the traps on that one.

The two bereaved dotards duetting in the kitchen? Great programming, great television.

So how about a catastrophe-themed CD and video to emulate
hopefully last Christmas's 'Light A Candle For An Angel'?

Yeah, right. I hear what you're saying, Richard. You're saying, hey, where's this babe coming from? - and you're
absolutely right. But catastrophes happen all the time - we
can keep our fingers crossed.

Do you know who I mean by the blind girl from Chicken Shed?
Teamed up with someone of proven compassion savvy - Bob
Hoskins, say - she could do it for us on the day.

The girl from Chicken Shed and Bob could duet over footage
of this year's tragedies, such as they've been to date.

But, hey - hold the balloon, Richard! The balloon could
spoil the story. Imagine this scenario. The balloon takes
off. Six tots drown in a reservoir. The balloon crashes.
Who remembers the tots?

Let's make money!
Yours,
Liz

Liz Reed.

Directors: Jeff Boyd Liz Reed Martin Jacques
Simon King, Angela Picano (Sicily)
Registered in England NO: 2905691

Heart Felt Productions Limited

'A Tragedy Aired is a Tragedy Shared'

Garry Bushell
The Sun
Virginia Street
London E1 9BZ

Suites 139/140
Elm Park Mansions
Park Walk
LONDON
SW10 0AS

22nd August 1997

Tel: 0171-352-9689
Fax: 0171-376-8378

Dear Garry

'TOPLESS GLADIATORS!'

Ordinary 'Gladiators'? Per-lease! You remember the old after dinner game, Garry? 'You Want, You'd Settle For, You Get'?

You want to see Scorpio and Zodiac wrestling naked on a sea of foam.

You'd settle for seeing a provincial policewoman running around in her knickers.

You end up watching two fat men with squeaky voices firing ping-pong balls at one another.

True or what, Garry?

Here's the answer! 'Topless Gladiators' shortly to be pitched to the Fantasy Channel. We're currently auditioning top tottie from Samantha Bond and Yvonne Paul, but we're looking for a really cool presenter.

That's you, Garry! You'd be ideal. Vulgar without being irreverent. Are you up for it? Let me know!

Yours,

Liz

Liz Reed

Directors: Jeff Boyd Liz Reed Martin Jacques
Simon King, Angela Picano (Sicily)
Registered in England NO: 2905691

Heart Felt Productions Limited

'A Tragedy Aired is a Tragedy Shared'

Mike Hollingworth
Venture Artistes
Cuddesdon House
Cuddesdon
Oxford OS44 9HB

Suites 139/140
Elm Park Mansions
Park Walk
LONDON
SW10 0AS

28th August 1997

Tel: 01713252-9689
Fax: 0171-376-8378

Dear Mike
'<u>TOPLESS GLADIATORS!</u>'

We're about to conceptualise the above development to the Fantasy Channel. It is to be fronted by Garry Bushell and we are busy auditioning top babes from Samantha Bond and Yvonne Paul.

We think - and Garry agrees with us - that your client, His Honour, Judge James Pickles, would be really mega-great as arbitrator.

"Topless contestants! You will go on my first whistle!" "Topless Gladiators! You will go on my second whistle!"

Fly this one past James, willya? If he's up for it, let me know soonest so I can attach his name to the pitch.

And, hey, chuck me a ball park figure for a sixty minute pilot, ditto what he'd want if it went to series.

Be nice!

Yours,

Liz

Liz Reed.

Directors: Jeff Boyd Liz Reed Martin Jacques
Simon King, Angela Picano (Sicily)
Registered in England NO: 2905691

VENTURE ARTISTES

Monday, September 29, 1997

Liz Reed,
Heartfelt Productions,
Suites 139/140,
Elm Park Mansions,
Park Walk,
London SW10 0AS.

Dear Liz,

My apologies for the delay in getting this note to you re. James Pickles and the topless gladiators idea.

As I told you on my phone message, James is most happy, in principle, to allow his name to go forward with this proposal. If at some stage you feel you can let us have a copy of the outline commitment we would be able to give you a ball park figure of his fees. (Obviously, we need to have an idea of what is required before we can quote!)

We would assume that this is a location-based project with all travel and expenses taken care of – it would then be a question of time required and number of shows within that time period.

Look forward to hearing from you.

Kind regards,

Mike Hollingsworth

Venture artistes-Universal Phone: 07000 402001; Universal Fax: 07000 402002; Mobile: 0836 637086
Postal Address: Cuddesdon House, Cuddesdon, Oxford OX 44 9HB. E-MAIL: venture- artistes@msn.com
Venture Television Ltd. trading as: Venture Artistes, Venture Broadcasting

Heart Felt Productions Limited

'A Tragedy Aired is a Tragedy Shared'

Paul Dunthorne
The Fantasy Channel
Portland House
Portland Place
London E14.

Suites 13/140
Elm Park Mansions
Park Walk
LONDON
SW10 0AS

23rd October 1997

Tel: 0171-352-9689
Fax: 0171-376-8378

Dear Paul

'TOPLESS GLADIATORS!'

Hey - no reaction yet to my colleague Liz
Reed's pitch of 28th August.

I'm very much in second chair on this one, but
Liz is in Singapore this afternoon so I'm just
touching base on her behalf.

In my judgement, this development could really
turn things round for your channel. We have Jo
'Be My' Guest and Nikki Diamond (former
Gladiator, Rhino) as topless babes, Garry
Bushell as co-presenter and His Honour Judge
James Pickles as arbitrator.

But hey, Paul, if you want to pass on all that
just give me the nod and I'll lob it over to
Kevin at Live TV.

So - in your court.

Best.

Jeff Boyd.

Directors: Jeff Boyd Liz Reed Martin Jacques
Simon King, Angela Picano (Sicily)
Registered in England NO: 2905691

TO: Jeff Boyd

OF: Heart Felt Productions

FROM: Paul Dunthorne

NUMBER: 0171 376 8378 **FAX COVER SHEET**

DATE: 28/10/97

Number of pages including this one: 1

Dear Mr Boyd

Thank you for your letter dated 23rd October regarding "Topless Gladiators".

I would be interested in seeing a budget breakdown of the said enterprise. In addition to this I could need to see a programme breakdown, step by step guide as to what everyone will be doing throughout the show and why. I would also need to see how you will address the copyright issues involved here.

Your casting seems a little odd on first glance (an old woman, a woman who has probably never done a press up in her life and two fat old men). No doubt this will become clear when you send me a programme breakdown and we establish whom is doing what.

I look forward to hearing from you.

Yours sincerely

Paul Dunthorne
Programme controller

Heart Felt Productions Limited

'A Tragedy Aired is a Tragedy Shared'

Paul Dunthorne	Suites 139/140
The Fantasy Channel	Elm Park Mansions
Portland Place	Park Walk
London E14 9TT	LONDON SW10 0AS

29th October 1997

Tel: 0171-352-9689
Fax: 0171-376-8378

Dear Paul

TOPLESS GLADIATORS!'

Jeff has passed on your fax of 28th October. Our
Miss Picano (Sicily) is working on a budget breakdown now and I'll send you a copy on completion.

I can't make head nor tail of your final paragraph,
Paul. You refer to two fat women, a woman who has
never done a press-up in her life and two fat old
men.

By two fat women do you mean Jo 'Be My' Guest, the
Page 3 Stunna, and Nikki Diamond, former Gladiator
Rhino?

Surely not (photos enclosed). Jo 'Be My' Guest's
name literally spells 'Scorcher' and what if
Gladiator Nikki got you in a head scissors? As good
as it gets, yeah?

I agree that His Honour Judge Pickles is a fat old
man, but Garry Bushell? Garry is heavily built, but
not fat, and not a crumbly by a long chalk.

I can only think that my dippy secretary must have
accessed the wrong development, sending you 'ANGLO-
TRASH', another of our mega-concepts, instead of

'TOPLESS GLADIATORS'.

Directors: Jeff Boyd Liz Reed Martin Jacques
Simon King, Angela Picano (Sicily)
Registered in England NO: 2905691

The former does contain a seriously funny 'out-take'
from an exercise video featuring Vanessa Feltz and
Jeremy Isaacs. Perhaps that's what you're referring to.
It also contains 'footage' of a Bournemouth mystic who
claims to read Royal horoscopes by means of colonic
irrigation. I think my secretary must have sent you this
one.
Would you like to see the rest of it?
Have a great one!

Yours,

Liz

Liz Reed.

Directors: Jeff Boyd Liz Reed Martin Jacques
Simon King, Angela Picano (Sicily)
Registered in England NO: 2905691

Heart Felt Productions Limited

'A Tragedy Aired is a Tragedy Shared'

Garry Bushell
The Sun
Virginia Street
London E1 9BZ

29th October 1997

Suites 139/140
Elm Park Mansions
Park Walk
LONDON
SW10 0AS
Tel: 0171-352-9689
Fax: 0171-376-8378

Dear Garry

'<u>TOPLESS GLADIATORS!</u>'

Hi there! It's me again! You'll have been wondering why you haven't heard from me since our conversation back in August. Well! Perhaps the enclosed correspondence will explain.

This Dunthorne guy from the Fantasy Channel, where's he coming from, Garry? Do you have a 'history' of some sort with him? I can't figure out whether he's serious or some sort of wind-up merchant.

What do you reckon, Garry?

All the best.

Yours,

Liz

Liz

Directors: Jeff Boyd Liz Reed Martin Jacques
Simon King, Angela Picano (Sicily)
Registered in England NO: 2905691

1 Virginia Street, London EP1 9XP. Telephone: 0171 782 4000. Fax 0171 782 5605/0171-488 3253

'5/11

Dear Liz,

Thanks for your letter. I'm not surprised the Fantasy Channel are mucking you about — they are notorious dickheads.

Why not approach Granada's Men & Motors, or Bravo? More together, more viewers, no scummy porno links...

All the best

Garry (13 stne)

Registered Office: News Group Newspapers Ltd., P.O.Box495, Virginia Street, London E1 9XY.
Registered No: 679215 England

Heart Felt Productions Limited

'A Tragedy Aired is a Tragedy Shared'

Richard Branson
Virgin Records
Kensall House
553 Harrow Road
London W8
2nd September 1997

Suites 139/140
Elm Park Mansions
Park Walk
LONDON
SW10 0AS
Tel: 0171-352-9689
Fax: 0171-376-8378

Dear Richard

'DIANA - THE PEOPLE'S PRINCESS.'

Okay - bin mine of 15th August. This is the big one.
This is the one we've been waiting for.

Here's my immediate take. A musical tribute on CD and
video featuring a Di look-alike in heaven, serenaded
tastefully by her showbiz pals on earth. I've impacted
with Wayne Sleep, Billy Connolly, Mr Motivator,
Christopher Biggins, Lord Deedes and Michael Barrymore
(the troubled comedian) and they're all up for it.

Alas, I can't get Elton John to affirmatise at this
moment in time. He's taking the tragedy particularly
badly, of course. The pressure on him is even heavier
than it is on Bob Geldof, who also met Di on a couple
of occasions.

It will be a long healing process for Elton and Bob,
I'm afraid.

Not to worry - properly promoted, this one will <u>walk</u>
out of the shops, believe me. It will make last
year's Christmas compassion single - 'Light A Candle
For An Angel' - look like a shelf-filler. And that
was <u>big</u>.

Hey - let's make a record!

Yours,

Liz

Liz Reed.

Directors: Jeff Boyd Liz Reed Martin Jacques
Simon King, Angela Picano (Sicily)
Registered in England NO: 2905691

HEART FELT PRODUCTIONS

Suites 139-140
Elm Park Mansion
Park Walk
London SW10 0AS

Tel: 0171 352 9689
Fax: 0171 376 8378

Directors:
Steve Oboto
Ainsley Parrott
Winston Obogo
Simon Durity
P. Amin

Richard Branson
Virgin Records
Kensal House
553 Harrow Road
London W8

27th October 1997

Dear Richard

'<u>DIANA, THE PEOPLE'S PRINCESS</u>'.

Hey, my man, no reply to mine of 2nd September.

This isn't a black thing, is it? Yes, sir, that's
the truth, we're all black here, the brothers have
taken over.

But that don't signify we mean to play no race card.
No sir. That ain't our shit. The race card - well,
that's honky white shit. We're just looking for the
usual courtesies, my man.

So you get your sorry white arse into gear and let's
make a video!

Peace, my man!

Winston Obogo.

Virgin Management Ltd

120 Campden Hill Road, London W8 7AR
Tel: 0171-229 1282 Fax: 0171-727 8200

Mr Winston Obogo
HEART FELT PRODUCTIONS LTD
Suites 139/140
Elm Park Mansions
Park Walk
London
SW10 0AS

3rd November 1997

Dear Mr Obogo

Thank you for contacting Richard Branson.

This is to acknowledge safe receipt of your letter. Unfortunately, due to his heavy work schedule he is unable to respond to all his mail as promptly as he would like to.

However, either our office or one of the other Virgin Companies will be in touch as soon as possible.

Kind Regards

Sue Hale.

Sue Hale
Richard Branson's Office

Registered Office : 120 Campden Hill Road, London W8 7ar, Registered in England No.1568894

THE DEANERY
9 Amen Court
London
EC4M 7BU

Tel: 0171-236 2827
Fax: 0171-332 0298

From: The Dean of St Paul's
          The Very Revd Dr John Moses

FAX

17th September 1997

Liz Reed
Heart Felt Productions Limited
Suites 139/140
Elm Park Mansions
Park Walk
SW10 0AS

Dear Ms Reed

Thank you for your two letters addressed to the Dean.

I shall be glad to have a response to the two messages I have left on your answerphone in the course of the last ten days asking you to phone me. If you would care to ring me we can have a word about the Dean's involvement in the video you are producing in memory of Diana, Princess of Wales.

Yours sincerely,

Mrs Anita Butt
Secretary to the Dean

Heart Felt Productions Limited

'A Tragedy Aired is a Tragedy Shared'

Mrs Butt
The Deanery
9 Amen Corner
London EC4M 7BU

21st September 1997

Suites 139/140
Elm Park Mansions
Park Walk
LONDON
SW10 0AS
Tel: 0171-352-9689
Fax: 0171-376-8378

Dear Mrs Butt

'<u>DIANA, THE PEOPLE'S PRINCESS. LEST WE FORGET</u>.'

Hey - really great to get your fax with the news that the Dean is up for our Christmas compassion video. Sorry we were slow to answer the phone, but there's something we don't like to mention. We're all disabled here at Heart Felt, but we prefer not to make an 'issue' of it. Our telephonist, Mandy, has a speech impediment, so we communicate by mail.

That's enough about our problems. Here's how the video is shaping up. We'd like the Dean to open the show, either with an original tribute (not too solemn) or with the off-the-cuff remarks he made at the time of the tragedy.

Chris de Burgh will then sing 'There's a New Star in Heaven Tonight', followed by anecdotes (some sad, some humorous) from the Princess's showbiz friends - Lord Deedes, Richard Branson, Billy Connolly, Wayne Sleep, Christopher Biggins and Michael Barrymore (the troubled comedian).

Lest we forget that there were other tragedies during the year, Esther Rantzen and a group of grieving mothers will then recite prayers over footage of catastrophes (pensioners over a cliff, tots force-fed Ecstasy by playground fiends, whatever).

The finale will be more upbeat, with various bands playing Diana's fave music: techno, real, handbag house, garage, hip hop, drum 'n' bass etc. A few closing words from the Dean, perhaps, and then the credits.
You know what? I think we gotta show!
Break a leg, Mrs Butt!

Yours,

Liz

Liz Reed.

Directors: Jeff Boyd Liz Reed Martin Jacques
Simon King, Angela Picano (Sicily)
Registered in England NO: 2905691

THE DEANERY
9 AMEN Court
London
ECM 7BU

Tel: 0171-236 2827
Fax: 0171-332 0298

From: The Dean of St Paul's
The Very Revd Dr John Moses

2nd October 1997

Liz Reed
Heart Felt Productions Limited
Suites 139/140
Elm Park Mansions
Park Walk
SW10 0AS

Dear Liz

Thank you for your letter of 21st September.

May I confirm that I am agreeable to contributing to the video you are planning to produce in memory of Diana, Princess of Wales in the way you request. I would prefer to record a new message for the video and assume that this would be something around one to one-and-a-half minutes. I would of course need to see the video before recording and must ask you to give me good notice when you want to arrange to do the filming.

With best wishes,

Yours sincerely

John Moses

Dictated by the Dean
and signed in his absence

Heart Felt Productions Limited

'A Tragedy Aired is a Tragedy Shared'

Caroline Elliot
Radio 4
Broadcasting House
London W1A 1AA

Suites 139/140
Elm Park Mansions
Park Walk
LONDON
SW10 0AS

15th August 1997

Tel: 0171-352-9689
Fax: 0171-376-8378

Dear Caroline

'<u>WITH FRIENDS LIKE THIS . . . . . .</u>!'

Hi there! Listen – I recently pitched the above concept to James Boyle and he completely liked it!

However, he did say that it might be better pitched to his Commissioning Editor – and, hey, that's you, Caroline!

So this is the idea. Someone who has been very much at the wrong end of the media spotlight (we suggest Jeremy Isaacs) is given a chance to answer his critics. Plus, his friends are invited to speak up on his behalf.

But are they really his friends? Things start to go horribly wrong . . .!

If that's a little too 'cutting-edge' for the new, dumbed down Radio 4, what about something with Sue Gaisford? Perhaps she could join a panel of critics to take over from 'Pick Of The Week'?

Have a great one!

Yours,

Liz

Liz Reed.

Directors: Jeff Boyd Liz Reed Martin Jacques
Simon King, Angela Picano (Sicily)
Registered in England NO: 2905691

Heart Felt Productions Limited

'A Tragedy Aired is a Tragedy Shared'

Ian Chapman
Macmillan
25 Eccleston Place
London SW1W 9NF
15th September 1997

Suites 139/140
Elm Park Mansions
Park Walk
LONDON SW10 0AS
Tel: 0171-352-9689
Fax: 0171-376-8378

Dear Ian

Were you a mega-fan of Amy Jenkins's 'This Life' on BBC2?

I was. "Wow! That's _me_!" I used to think, and so did millions of other wash 'n' go, twentysomething babes.

Plus the one-liners literally made me die with laughter.

Miles to Anna (and is _she_ one smart lady!): "You don't want a relationship, Anna. You want to cut my balls off."

Anna: "That's if I can find them."

Hey, is that real or what?

Anyway – here's the goss: Penguin have bought volume rights in 'That's Life' and are looking for someone to novelise it. They've even approached – don't laugh! – Terence Blacker! Don't get me wrong, Ian. Terence is one helluva guy but he won't see 50 again – and 'This Life' is about _now_, yeah?

And here's the hottest goss: we've bought an original Amy Jenkins screenplay to be produced by us next spring. Entitled Is This Allowed?, it's a really scary take on sex, drugs and perversions in Ibiza, and a far more mature work than 'This Life'.

It would make a brilliant novel, and it might suit us to negotiate publishing rights now. Would you like to read the screenplay at this time, Ian? I'm sure you'd be as excited as we are.

With very best wishes.

Yours,

Liz

Liz Reed.

Directors: Jeff Boyd Liz Reed Martin Jacques
Simon King, Angela Picano (Sicily)
Registered in England NO: 2905691

2nd October 1997

Liz Reed
Heart Felt Productions Ltd
Suites 139/140
Elm Park Mansions
Park Walk
LONDON SW10 0AS

PAN

50 YEARS
Pan Books

25 Eccleston Place
London
SW1W 9NF

Tel: 0171 881 8000
Fax: 0171 881 8001

Dear Liz Reed

Ian Chapman passed me your letter of 15th September about Amy Jenkins and her new film script. Could you possibly give me some idea of plans for the film – especially any directors/producers lined up to work on it. We'd be happy to take a look at the screenplay for you but would need to know more about the scale of the project in order to assess the publishing potential of a novelisation.

I look forward to hearing from you shortly.

With best wishes
Yours

[signature]

Mari Evans

Pan celebrates fifty years

A Division of Pan Macmillan

Registered Office:
Brunel Road, Houndmills
Basinstoke
Hampshire RG21 6XS
Registered No: 785998 Engand

Heart Felt Productions Limited

'A Tragedy Aired is a Tragedy Shared'

The Rt Hon Michael Portillo
Conservative Association
Enfield/Southgate
814 Green Lanes
London N21 2SA
12th August 1997

Suites 139/140
Elm Park Mansions
Park Walk
LONDON SW10 0AS
0171-352-9689
Fax 0171 376 8078

Dear Michael

'<u>THE DAY MY WHOLE WORLD COLLAPSED</u>.'

OK, it's gone pear-shaped for Tragic TV Patsy Palmer. Broken romances have seen her turn to drink and drugs.

Showbiz pals say: "Her whole world collapsed when she was dumped by fiancé, Nick Love."

Now Tragic TV Patsy has booked herself into a drug and booze clinic dubbed 'The Palace of Pain'.

This company has been commissioned by the BBC to produce a discussion programme entitled 'THE DAY MY WHOLE WORLD COLLAPSED'. It will be chaired, we hope, by Tragic TV Patsy's celebrity therapist, TV Beechy Colclough. Others who may appear include Paul Merson, the troubled striker, and Tragic Bra Beauty, Sophie Anderton.

Experts will argue for the immediate legalisation of all drugs. As the voice of the new, caring, sharing, compassionate Tory Party, Michael, would you like to appear on the show in support of this argument?

Let me know, yeah? Filming in October.
Hey - just say "NO!" to drug hysteria!

Yours,

Liz

Liz Reed.

Directors: Jeff Boyd Liz Reed Martin Jacques
Simon King, Angela Picano (Sicily)
Registered in England NO: 2905691

HEART FELT PRODUCTIONS LIMITED

Suites 139-140
Elm Park Mansions
Park Walk
London SW10 0AS

Tel: 0171 352 9689
Fax: 0171 376 8378

Directors:
Steve Oboto
Ainsley Parrott
Winston Obogo
Simon Durity
P. Amin

19th October 1997

The Rt Hon Michael Portillo
Enfield Conservative Association
814 Green Lanes
London N21 2SA

Dear Michael

'THE DAY MY WHOLE WORLD COLLAPSED.'

Word up! It's gone pear-shaped for Tragic TV Patsy
Palmer. Broken romances have seen her turn to drink and
drugs.

Showbiz pals say: "Her whole world collapsed when she was
dumped by fiance, Nick Love."

Now Tragic TV Patsy has booked herself into a drug and
booze clinic dubbed 'The Palace of pain'.

OK, the brothers have been commissioned by the BBC to
produce a discussion programme entitled 'THE DAY MY WHOLE
WORLD COLLAPSED'. It will be chaired, we hope, by Tragic
TV Patsy's celebrity therapist, TV Beechy Colclough.
Others who may appear include Paul Merson, the troubled
striker, and Tragic Bra Beauty, Sophie Anderton.

Experts will argue for the immediate legalisation of all
drugs. As the choice of the new, caring, sharing, compassionate Tory Party, Michael, would you like to appear on
the show in support of this argument? Filming in
November.

Hey - give it up large in support of the brothers!

Peace, my man.

Winston Obogo

Winston Obogo.

FAX MESSAGE

From: RT Hon Micheal Portillo

To: Winston Obogo

Date:

Subject: The Day My Whole World.

Pages to follow: 0

Message:

It was good to hear from you.

I am grateful to you for thinking
of me, but this one is not for me

With every good wish.

Michael.

If you have any difficulty in reading this fax, please call/fax back:
0171 8282550

Heart Felt Productions Limited

'A Tragedy Aired is a Tragedy Shared'

Jane Root
Independent Commissions
BBC Television
Wood Lane
London W12
16th September 1997

Suites 139/140
Elm Park Mansions
Park Walk
LONDON
SW10 0AS
Tel: 0171-352-9689
Fax: 0171-376-8378

Dear Jane

<u>'WHO PUT HEROIN IN MY KIDDIES' SWEETS?'</u>
Hi there! It's me again! Have you had time yet to critique the above, pitched in early August?

Your long deliberations make me think you're taking it really seriously! That's great!

There have been some mega-brilliant developments since I wrote. Jane Butterworth, the News of the World's experienced Agony Aunt, will preside over a dramatised version of 'Jane's Photo-File'.

Sir Bernard Ingham has agreed to front 'POPPYCOCK!', as the Man Whose Bite Is Worse Than His Bark!

In a section entitled 'DON'T LEAVE IT ALL TO BOOTS THE CHEMIST! GET A LOVED ONE INTO TROUBLE!', Edward Enfield, the consumer sneak, will man the Heart Felt Grass-Up Line.

"Hullo Mrs Bassett. Can you hear me?"

"Very much so, thank you Edward."

"Good. Do you want to get a loved one into trouble?"

"Very much so, Edward. My 90-year-old gran, who suffers from arthritis, is growing a cannabis plant in her window box."

"Leave it to us, Mrs Bassett. Have you enjoyed appearing on the show?"

"Very much so, Edward."
Great TV or what, Jane?
Input us soonest, yeah.
Yours,

Liz

Liz Reed.

Directors: Jeff Boyd Liz Reed Martin Jacques
Simon King, Angela Picano (Sicily)
Registered in England NO: 2905691

Heart Felt Productions Limited

'A Tragedy Aired is a Tragedy Shared'

Karen Black
LOOK-ALIKES
13 Cinnamon Row
Plantation Wharf
London SW11 3TW
16th September 1997

Suites 139/140
Elm Park Mansions
Park Walk
LONDON
SW10 0AS
Tel: 0171-352-9689
Fax: 0171-376-8378

Dear Karen
'JANE'S PHOTO-FILE'

Many thanks for sending me photos of your artistes. They look a fine lot!

However, none of them on the face of it looks exactly right for a part in 'JANE'S PHOTO-FILE'. Nor, I must admit, was I aware that you only represented look-alikes. It must be kinda weird constantly being mistaken for Shakespeare or Einstein when you're out shopping. You're at the meat counter in Waitrose, someone comes up to you and says:

"Hey! I know you! You're Shakespeare!"

Or they come up to you and say:

"Hey! I know you! You're Einstein!"

Does Dr Watson get much work? Less than Shakespeare or Einstein, that's my guess. My guess is that if a member of the general public went up to Dr Watson in a supermarket they'd say:

"Who in the name of arse are you?"

My girlfriend doesn't agree. She reckons Dr Watson gets just as much work as Shakespeare or Einstein. Could you settle this dispute, Karen?
Do you have a Princess Di look-alike on your books? If you do, she might be suitable for another of our developments. We are progressing a Christmas compassion tribute to the tragic Princess and are actively looking for an artiste to play her on film.
Let me know if you have a Diana look-alike, Karen.
Have a great one!

Yours,

Liz

Liz Reed.

NEWS OF THE **WORLD**

1 VIRGINIA STREET, LONDON, E1 9XR
Telephone: 0171-782 1000
Fax: 0171-583 9504

THE WORLDS LARGEST SUNDAY SALE

Liz Reed
Heart Felt Productions
Suites 139-140
Elm Park Mansions
Park Walk
London SW10 0AS

15 September 1997

Dear Liz

Many thanks for your letter. The programme sounds a great idea and I am writing to confirm that I would indeed be interested in taking part, subject to the News of the World's approval.

I'd like to know a little more. What age is your target audience? Are you pitching at simply tabloid readers or to a wider audience? What is the general tone to be? Are the problems to be acted out absolutely straight? Will the advice be straight? What sort of problems are you interested in? Who selects the problems? Do you have any idea when you will start shooting?

I think trying to buy the TV broadcast rights from the NOTW would be an enormous hassle. A better idea, I feel, would be for me to write new ones or adapt ones that I have already written – after all, there are only so many problems as each picture story is only very loosely based on letters I recieve and writing new ones would not be a problem. At the moment I try and keep the dialogue as sharp and snappy as possible to fit in with the six frames, so they would need to be expanded slightly for television format. QED, I might as well write new ones.
I can't see that the NOTW would object – I have done countless TV appearances before, but this is a little different as it involved giving advice so I will need to run it past them as per my contract.

Look forward to hearing from you
Best wishes

JANE BUTTERWORTH

Registered Office: News Group NewspapersLtd., P.O.Box495, Virginia Street, London E1 9XY
Registered No: 679251 England

Heart Felt Productions Limited

'A Tragedy Aired is a Tragedy Shared'

Martin Bell MP
The House of Commons
London SW1.

20th September 1997

Suites 139/140
Elm Park Mansions
Park Walk
LONDON SW10 0AS
Tel: 0171-352 9689
Fax: 0171-376-8378

Dear Martin
'<u>DON'T LEAVE IT TO BOOTS THE CHEMIST! GET A LOVED ONE INTO
TROUBLE!</u>'

Hi there! Listen - we've been commissioned by the BBC to
pilot 'WHO PUT HEROIN IN MY KIDDIES' SWEETS?', an exciting
take on tabloid values brought to the TV screen.

A featured high-point of the show will be a section entitled 'DON'T LEAVE IT ALL TO BOOTS THE CHEMIST! GET A LOVED
ONE INTO TROUBLE!' Members of the general public will be
encouraged to 'shop' their nearest and dearest down the
Heart Felt Grass-Up Line for using substances specifically
banned by New Labour.

Vaseline. Vibrators. Bananas. Novelty knickers. Strap-on
dildos. Baco-foil, Bunsen burners. Polaroid cameras. You
name it.

"My old gran spent her Giro on a corset!" "I found a see-
through blouse in my daughter-in-law's wardrobe!" That sort
of thing, yeah.

Anyway, Martin, Jane Root, our Exec Producer at the BBC, is
keen that the Grass-Up Line Mediator should be whiter than
white in his personal arrangements.

Here's what Jane said at our last meeting. "What we don't
want, Liz," she said, "is for our Grass-Up Line Mediator to
be found with an envelope from a Muslim shopkeeper in his
pocket or on the kitchen table with a satzuma up his arse."

Absolutely right. He must be impeccable, yeah. Well, we
think that means you or Edward Enfield, and everyone we've
researched it with agrees with us.

"For me," everyone says, "it must be Edward Enfield, the
consumer sneak, or Martin Bell MP."

Will you man our Grass-Up Line, Martin?

Hey - let's get some people into trouble!
Yours,

Liz

Liz Reed,

Directors: Jeff Boyd Liz Reed Martin Jacques
Simon King, Angela Picano (Sicily)
Registered in England NO: 2905691

30 Oct 97

Dear Liz Reed,

I am sorry not to have got back to you sooner.
It sounds a great project — but, alas, I am simply too
busy to be able to help you. My diary is under siege,
and a regular TV programme would take ~~up~~ up much
more time than I have. I'm sorry.

Best wishes

Martin Bell

Heart Felt Productions Limited

'A Tragedy Aired is a Tragedy Shared'

Steve Hewlett
Channel 4 Television
124 Horseferry Road
London SW1P 2TX

21st September 1997

Dear Steve

<u>'ANGLOTRASH!'</u>

Suites 139/140
Elm Park Mansions
Park Walk
LONDON
SW10 0AS
Tel: 0171-352-9689
Fax: 0171-376-8378

Congratulations from everyone at Heart Felt on your new job! Really great!

Here's the word: as you'll know, 'ANGLOTRASH' has been a mega-hit in France for Canal Plus, and we've optioned the UK rights. At the moment, and in conjunction with Avalon, we're putting cod English voice-overs on to the footage which literally creased them in France. Some of it's mega-sensitive, as you'd expect (security and the Duchess of York's colonic irrigator are two concepts which have yet to make each other's acquaintance!), but, just to give you a taste, we do have pirated footage of:

Suffolk mothers stuffing midgets into Christmas crackers!
Oiled mountain women wrestling in Cornish coves!
Mad dapple-bottomed women in Bournemouth clinics claiming to cure baldness by manipulation of the sexual organs!

Plus we have:

Michael Winner watering his garden in a posing pouch!
Vanessa Feltz testing a flatulence-free baked bean!
Clive James learning to salsa dance with Elle Macpherson (arse out to contain erection)!

We have footage of Janet Street-Porter, Steve!

So, waddya say? I'll bike you round a tape when we've finished the voice-overs, yeah. As Karen Krisanovitch says in today's in ya face Independent:

"It's dollars <u>uber alles</u>, baby!"
Ciao for now!

Liz

Liz Reed. Directors: Jeff Boyd Liz Reed Martin Jacques
Simon King, Angela Picano (Sicily)
Registered in England NO: 2905691

CHANNEL FOUR TELEVISION   124 HORSEFERRY ROAD, LONDON SW1P 2TX
TELEPHONE: 0171-396-4444. DIRECT LINE: 0171-306 8700
FAX: 0171-306 8356.
MINICOM: 0171-306 8691
EMAIL: JPARTRIDGE@CHANNEL4.CO.UK

1st October 1997

Liz Reed
Heart Felt Productions
Suites 139/140
Elm Park Mansions
Park Walk
London
SW10 0AS

Dear Liz

<u>Re: Anglotrash</u>

Thanks for your proposal which was received this week by Channel 4.

As you know Steve Hewlett has been appointed as the new incoming Head Factual
Programmes & Features. He arrived at Channel 4 this week and inevitably it will take
some time for him to set out his stall. However, it's worth bearing in mind that the
Head of Department role is not a commissioning one and Steve will have no signifi-
cant budget to spend on original programming. Mostly he will oversee the output of
the various departments that fall within his remit and guide projects in the right direc-
tion.

In this case your project seems most appropriate to Channel 4's Entertainment
Department and you should approach either its new head, Kevin Lygo, when he starts
later this month, or commissioning editor Entertainment, Graham K Smith. This might
seem frustrating – after all it could go in the internal post – but in a busy and demand-
ing work environment there is no substitute for pitching directly to the person with the
budget to spend.

Best wishes

<u>Jane Partridge</u>
Editorial Administrator
Factual & Features

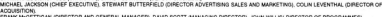
CHANNEL FOUR TELEVISION
SIR MICHAEL BISHOP CBE (CHAIRMAN), DAVID PLOWRIGHT(DEPUTY CHAIRMAN)
MICHAEL JACKSON (CHIEF EXECUTIVE), STEWART BUTTERFIELD (DIRECTOR ADVERTISING SALES AND MARKETING), COLIN LEVENTHAL (DIRECTOR OF
ACQUISITION).
FRANK McGETTIGAN (DIRECTOR AND GENERAL MANAGER), DAVID SCOTT (MANAGING DIRECTOR), JOHN WILLIS(DIRECTOR OF PROGRAMMES).
SECRETARY: ANDREW YEATES

Heart Felt Productions Limited

'A Tragedy Aired is a Tragedy Shared'

Jane Partridge
Channel 4 Television
124 Horseferry Road
London SW1 2TX

Suites 139/140
Elm Park Mansions
Park Walk
LONDON
SW10 0AS

3rd October 1997

Tel: 0171-352-9689
Fax: 0171-376-8378

Dear Jane

'<u>ANGLOTRASH!</u>'

Hey – <u>*mega*</u>-thanks for your brilliant letter of 1st October. <u>Really</u>.

I won't go on or you'll think I'm really sad.

"Wow – what's wrong with this babe," you'll think. "She should get a life."

It's just that it's so rare to find a really caring person in this cut-throat business, a person who has sufficient self-esteem to be there for others.

Do you know Jane Root? I *mean*!

Anyway – I'm taking your advice and pitching 'ANGLOTRASH' to Graham K Smith.

I really hope he likes it. And thanks again. I've got a feeling that you're a really nice person.

Yours,

Liz

Liz Reed.

Directors: Jeff Boyd Liz Reed Martin Jacques
Simon King, Angela Picano (Sicily)
Registered in England NO: 2905691

Heart Felt Productions Limited

'A Tragedy Aired is a Tragedy Shared'

Alan Marke   Suites 139/140
Channel X   Elm Park Mansions
22 Stephenson Way   Park Walk
London NW1 2HD   LONDON
                                  SW10 0AS
2nd October 1997   Tel: 0171-352-9689
                                  Fax: 0171-376-8378

Dear Alan

Hi there! Congratulations on 'SHOOTING STARS'! Vic and Bob
get wackier and wackier. Everyone's agreed on that. "For me,"
everyone says, "no one is wackier than Vic and Bob. Not even
Chris Evans is wackier than Vic and Bob!"
"Trav . . . . . . aaaaaaaaaaa . . . .nooooooooooooooo!"

"Ev . . . . . . aaaaaaaaaaaaaa . . . . . . noooooooo!"

Yeah really, you guys up at Channel X understand comedy. At
Heart Felt we understand tragedy.

We're developing a Christmas video as a tribute to Diana,
Princess of Wales. But we don't want it to be all doom and
horror. Di had a terrific sense of humour and would have been
the first to see the funny side of what happened.

"What's the Queen giving Fergie for Christmas?"
"I don't know."
"Dinner for two at the Paris Ritz!"

Diana would have led the laughter.

We've booked a lot of mainstream talent – the Dean of St
Paul's, Michael Barrymore (the troubled comedian), Bill
Deedes, Wayne Sleep etc – but we need something zany.
(Richard Branson is doing a skit with Gazza in which they
both wear women's bosoms outside their shirts (!) but we
need something even zanier than that.)

Would you guys co-produce and persuade Vic and Bob to par-
ticipate?
Ev . . . . . aaaaaaaaaaaaa . . . . . . noooooooo!
Have a great one!
Yours,

Liz

Liz Reed.   Directors: Jeff Boyd Liz Reed Martin Jacques
                     Simon King, Angela Picano (Sicily)
                     Registered in England NO: 2905691

3rd October 1997

Liz Reed
Heart Felt Productions Limited
Suites 139/140
Elm Park Mansions
Park Walk
London SW10 0AS

Dear Liz

Thank you for your letter.

Unfortunately Vic Reeves & Bob Mortimer are too busy
to contribute to your project.

Good luck with the Christmas Video.

Yours sincerely,

Alan Marke

CHANNEL X COMMUNICATIONS LIMITED
22 STEPHENSON WAY LONDON NW1 2HD
TEL 0171 387 3874 FAX 0171 387 0738
REGISTERED IN ENGLAND N° 2910884

ginger

Air Limited

Liz Reed
Heart Felt Productions Ltd
Suites 139/140
Elm Park Mansions
Park Walk
London
SW10 0AS
12 November 1997

Dear Liz

Thank you very much for taking the time to send me your programme proposal
for a Christmas compassion video as a tribute to Diana, Princess of Wales.
Unfortunately, Ginger Productions development state is currently full, so we
are not taking on any further proposals at present.

Sadly, Chris will also be too busy to contribute to your production. What with
his Virgin Breakfast Show and TFI Friday, there are not enough hours in the
day! May I wish you every success with your project and best wishes for the
future.

Yours sincerely

Jools Barringer
Assistant to Chris Evans

The Media Centre, 3rd Floor, 131-151 Great Titchfield Street, London W1P 6DB
tel: 0171-577 7100 fax: 0171-577 7135
Ginger air Ltd director chris evans, registered in england company no 3023038
registered office: paramount house, 102-170 Wardour street, london W1V 3a6

RADIO

BRITISH BROADCA
STING CORPORATION
BROADCASTING HOUSE
PORTLAND PLACE
LONDON W1A 1AA
TELEPHONE:0171 580 4468

Ms Liz Reed,
Heart Felt Productions Limited,
Suites 139/140,
Elm Park Mansions,
Park Walk,
London. SW10 0AS   24th September 1997

Dear Ms Reed,

Thank you for your letter of 2nd September.

I did, in fact, reply to your letter of 15th August on 20th August – copy attached.

In place of 'Pick of the Week' we will be providing an 'arts' programme which will include daily arts news and more considered arts journalism.

For this commissioning round, Radio 4 has invited independent producers to submit proposals on the basis of a number of factors, in particular, available slots, genres and track record. Let me assure you that those companies who have been unsuccessful in this round will be invited to offer proposals in future commissioning rounds.

In the meantime, I will keep your company on file and if you are interested in submitting any proposals perhaps you could let me know.

With best wishes.

Yours sincerely,

(Caroline Elliot)
Network Manager, Radio

Heart Felt Productions Limited

'A Tragedy Aired is a Tragedy Shared'

Caroline Elliot
BBC Radio 4
Broadcasting House
London W1A 1AA

Suites 139/140
Elm Park Mansions
Park Walk
LONDON
SW10 0AS

4th October 1997

Tel: 0171-352-9689
Fax: 0171-376-8378

Dear Caroline,

Oh bum! I <u>knew</u> I shouldn't have mentioned Sue
Gaisford!

I've now dropped her from the pilot, but too late for
you, it seems. Never mind. I'll put it down to experience.

Anyway, it's brilliant to know that we're 'ON FILE'
and that you'll be inviting us to offer proposals in
future commissioning rounds.

We'll continue to progress 'WITH FRIENDS LIKE THIS .
. . . . .' (if we can find someone, <u>anyone </u>(!) to
speak up for Jeremy Isaacs - no luck yet) and we'll
not be slow with other suggestions. I assure you!
(Nothing with Sue Gaisford!)

All the best, Caroline.

Yours,

Liz

Liz Reed.

Directors: Jeff Boyd Liz Reed Martin Jacques
Simon King, Angela Picano (Sicily)
Registered in England NO: 2905691

BRITISH BROADCASTING CORPORATION
BROADCASTING HOUSE
PORTLAND PLACE
LONDON W1A 1AA
TELEPHONE:0171 580 4468

EXTENSION:
DIRECT LINE:
FAX:

7th October 1997

Liz Reed
Heart Felt Productions Ltd
Suites 139/140
Elm Park Mansions
Park Walk
London
SW10 0AS

Dear Liz

Please find attached copy of a letter sent to you on 23 September 1997.

As you can see, it is not a project that interests us so we would appreciate if you did not contact us again about this proposal.

Kind regards,

Alex Greenwood

Enc

BRITISH BROADCASTING CORPORATION
ROOM 3218
WHITE CITY
210 WOOD LANE
LONDON W12 7TS
TELEPHONE 0181-752 5252
EXTENSIONS: 25766, 26873, 26374
FAX: 0181-75204090

23rd September 1997

Liz Reed
Heart Felt Productions Ltd
Suite 139/140
Elm Park Mansions
Park Walk
London
SW10 0AS

Dear Liz

Thank you for sending your unusual proposal for a nightly magazine programme to Jane Root. Jane discussed your ideas with the other Executive Producers and, as Proposals Manager, I am now replying on their behalf.

At the moment we are looking for either ideas that could fill the gardening/food slots on BBC or documentary leisure ideas with a broad based appeal for BBC1. Unfortunately your idea would not fit easily into any of these slots so I'm afraid we won't be able to take up your idea at this time.

I am sorry to disappoint you and your ever-changing list of company directors.

Kind regards,

Alex Greenwood
Proposals Manager

Heart Felt Productions Limited

'A Tragedy Aired is a Tragedy Shared'

Alex Greenwood
BBC Television
Television Centre
Wood Lane
London W12 7RJ

Suites 139/140
Elm Park Mansions
Park Walk
LONDON
SW10 0AS

10th October 1997

Tel: 0171-352-9689
Fax: 0171-376-8378

Dear Alex,

Liz has gone to Hong Kong for the afternoon, so I'm responding on her behalf to yours of 3rd September.

Thanks for tipping us off to Jane's clean sweep of all BBC2's cookery and gardening slots.

It'll be a bit of a bombshell to some that you're dropping Delia after all these years. Has she been told yet? One door closes etc, but my guess is she'll be a bit upset.

The wally with the hot wok will be less of a loss, as will the grinning black pillock.

I have taken note of what I assume is a wise-crack in the final paragraph of your letter about our 'ever-changing list of company directors'.

We work the squad system here, Alex, like a successful football club, fielding such personnel as seem appropriate for the occasion.

Thank you for inviting us to pitch leisure ideas to BBC1. You will be hearing from us very soon.

All the best, Alex.
Yours,

Jeff Boyde

Directors: Marcus Plantin (Chairman) Geoff Attkinson Mark Chapman Peter Bennett-Jones Debbie Mason Linda Agran Justin Judd Jimmy Mulvill Jeff Boyde Liz Reed Angela Picano (Sicily)
Registered in England NO: 2905691

Heart Felt Productions Limited

'ON FILE WITH RADIO 4!'

Delia Smith
c/o Hawkshead
48 Bedford Square
London WC1

11th October 1997

Suites 139/140
Elm Park Mansions
Park Walk
LONDON
SW10 0AS
Tel: 0171-352-9689
Fax: 0171-376-8378

Dear Delia,

<u>Really</u> gutted to hear from Jane Root (she's Head of
Independent Commissions at the BBC) that she plans
a radical new look for all BBC2's cookery programmes and that yours is to be among the casual-
ties.

Never mind. This company is forging strong links
with Channel 5, thanks to my really great relationship with Dawn Airey.

OK, Dawn was a baby boomer and I'm Generation X,
yeah, but in spite of that we get on brilliantly.

I'm not saying that we'd be comfortable clubbing
together or getting on one on a Friday night, but
for an older chick she's cool. Plus our take on
what makes a ratings winner is usually the same.

Dawn is Controller of Programmes at Channel 5,
Delia, and very keen to raise the profile of their
leisure out-put. I've already had a word with her
about your unexpected availability and without
raising your hopes unnecessarily, I think I can say
that she'll want to take a meeting with you soonest.

So - don't get too downhearted!

Be nice!

Yours,

Liz Reed.

Directors: Jeff Boyd Liz Reed Martin Jacques
Simon King, Angela Picano (Sicily)
Registered in England NO: 2905691

SILLY WAITER

Mark Howard **LOOK ALIKES**
0171 720 0525 Fax: 0171 622 6366

CROCODILE DUNDEE

Sid Wragg **LOOK ALIKES**
0171 720 0525 Fax: 0171 622 6366

PRINCESS DIANA

Christina Hance **LOOK ALIKES**
0171 720 0525 Fax: 0171 622 6366

Heart Felt Productions Limited

'A Tragedy Aired is a Tragedy Shared'

Karen Black
Look Alikes
13 Cinnamon Row
Plantation Wharf
London SW11 3TW

Suites 139/140
Elm Park Mansions
Park Walk
LONDON
SW10 0AS

21st September 1997

Tel: 0171-352-9689
Fax: 0171-376-8378

Dear Karen

'<u>LEST WE FORGET</u>'

Thanks for yours of 18th September, enclosing photo of Christina Hance. She certainly looks the part. What's her daily rate?

We will probably want to film towards the end of next month – it's just a question of getting our various compassion artistes (Chris de Burgh, Clive James, Lord Deedes, Michael Barrymore – the troubled comedian) on side at the same time.

Hey, thanks, too, for enclosing photos of some of your other look-alikes. Nothing really suitable at the moment for Crocodile Dundee or Silly Waiter, but I'll keep them on file.

Let me know about Christina.

Yours,

Liz

Liz Reed.

Directors: Jeff Boyd Liz Reed Martin Jacques
Simon King, Angela Picano (Sicily)
Registered in England NO: 2905691

Heart Felt Productions Limited

'A Tragedy Aired is a Tragedy Shared'

Dawn Airey
Channel 5 Broadcasting
22 Long Acre
London WC2E 9LY

14th October 1997

Suites 139/140
Elm Park Mansions
Park Walk
LONDON
SW10 0AS
Tel: 0171-352-9689
Fax: 0171-376-8378

Dear Dawn
'<u>DISABLED GLADIATORS!</u>'

Hi there! It's me again! Hey – I was looking at the schedules yesterday, wondering why Channel 5 hadn't made any impact on the ratings, when I was literally struck by a BIG IDEA! Here was the evening's menu, Dawn:

BBC1. 7.30. A multiple sclerosis victim is sexually abused but the case is thrown out because she isn't a competent witness.

ITV. 8pm. A 9-year-old quadriplegic, who is dependent on a ventilator, graduates at Oxford University.

Channel 4. 9pm. Dr Jam Ghajar examines accident related coma victims and argues that severe head trauma occurs not on impact but when the brain starts to swell.

Had Esther not been temporarily replaced on BBC2 by the World Bowls Championship we would have been dealt a full hand of disaster programming.

What does that tell you, Dawn? It tells me that sassy, in ya face mega-babes like Julia Bradbury and fun guys like Jono Coleman and his tucker-box can't compete with catastrophe TV.

So – Heart Felt to the rescue! '<u>DISABLED GLADIATORS!</u>' Does that tighten your buns, Dawn? My guess is <u>yes</u>!

Legless Falklands hero, Corporal Bob 'Jumper' Cross, will co-present with mother-of-two Pru Stokes. Pru, you'll recall, made everyone laugh on 'ESTHER' when she explained why she was in a wheelchair. Her pet labrador knocked her backwards down a wishing-well! So there's a gal who hasn't lost her lovely sense of humour!
What do you think, Dawn? Input us soonest.
Cuuuuuuue Kirsty!

Yours,
Liz
Liz Reed.

Directors: Jeff Boyd Liz Reed Martin Jacques
Simon King, Angela Picano (Sicily)
Registered in England NO: 2905691

Dawn Airey
Director of Programmes

16 October 1997

Liz Reed
Heart Felt Productions Limited
Suites 139/140
Elm Park Mansions
Park Walk
London SW10 0AS

Dear Liz

Thank you for your recent letter.
I am afraid I do not agree with your assertions that we have not made a serious impact on the ratings. We are meeting our business plan and achieving our share predictions, but I am sure you will appreciate that with a modest programming budget, the Channel was never established to compete head on with the other terrestrial broadcasters.

I am sorry to advise you that DISABLED GLADIATORS is not an idea that I like and therefore I cannot progress it. You should also be aware that Channel 5 deals only with preferred suppliers: to be a preferred supplier you must have a successful track record in producing high quality, top rating, long running series on challenged budgets. With respect, I do not believe that your company matches these criteria.

Thank you for your continued interest in Channel 5.
With best wishes
Yours sincerely

Dawn Airey

Channel 5 Broadcasting Limited 22 Long Acre London WC23 9LY
Telephone : 0171 550 5555 Faxcimile: 0171 550 5554

Registered in England no: 3147460

Heart Felt Productions Limited

'A Tragedy Aired is a Tragedy Shared'

Dawn Airey
Channel 5 Broadcasting
22 Long Acre
London WC2E 9LY

Suites 139/140
Elm Park Mansions
Park Walk
LONDON
SW10 0AS

17th October 1997

Tel: 0171-352-9689
Fax: 0171-376-8378

Dear Dawn,

Well thanks a whole fucking <u>heap</u>!

My life's crap at the moment, frankly, I haven't had a holiday for two years, my cat, Mr Boots, died last week, my dealer's shagging my tax adviser, I'm <u>struggling</u> to get Heart Felt's act together and then I get your letter saying that this company doesn't come up to the required criteria.

So how do you think that made me feel, Dawn?

I'll tell you. It made me feel like shit. It made me feel utterly worthless. It was a real blow to my self-image. It made me want to stick my head down the toilet with the rest of my life.

I mean, what's the fucking <u>point</u>, Dawn?

That said, I may have something for you. Have you heard that Jane Root (she's Head of Independent Commissions at the BBC) is giving all BBC2's cookery and gardening programmes a long overdue face-lift?

What does that tell you, Dawn? It tells me that Delia Smith's available, and I've already been in touch with her people at Hawkshead, alerting them to my relationship with you and suggesting that, because of this, I could probably swing Delia a face-saving deal with Channel 5.

Exciting news or what?

I look forward to hearing from you, Dawn.

Have a great one!

Yours,

Liz Reed.

Directors: Jeff Boyd Liz Reed Martin Jacques
Simon King, Angela Picano (Sicily)
Registered in England NO: 2905691

Dawn Airey
Director of Programmes

22 October 1997

Liz Reed
Heart Felt Productions Limited
Suites 139/140
Elm Park Mansions
Park Walk
London
SW10 0AS

Dear Liz

Thank you for your emotional and rather abusive response to my letter dated 16 October. Such a reply is not going to endear you to a potential Broadcaster.

If you watch Channel 5 you will be aware that we have deliberately avoided poaching high profile clients from other Broadcasters and whilst Delia Smith is clearly an extremely popular cook, I am not too sure she would be right for Channel 5. However, should you secure her services then I am sure Michael Attwell, Controller of Features and Arts would be interested in having an initial conversation with you.

Yours sincerely

Dawn Airey

c.c. Michael Attwell

Channel 5 Broadcasting Limited 22 Long Acre London WC23 9LY
Telephone : 0171 550 5555 Faxcimile: 0171 550 5554

Registered in England no: 3147460

Heart Felt Productions Limited

`'A Tragedy Aired is a Tragedy Shared'`

Dawn Airey
Channel 5 Broadcasting
22 Long Acre
London WC2E 9LY

24th October 1997

Suites 139/140
Elm Park Mansions
Park Walk
LONDON
SW10 0AS
Tel: 0171-352-9689
Fax: 0171-376-8378

Dear Dawn,
You're absolutely right. Mine of 16th October was <u>way</u> out of order.

It's the old story. I tried to be everything to everybody and ended up being nothing to myself. Now I realise that I'm at a place in my life when I must focus on <u>me</u>. I must learn to be happy with who I am and with what I'm doing.

Hopefully, when I have a positive perception of myself, when I can look in the mirror and say, "Hey! I like <u>me</u>!", I'll be less easily upset by the negative attitudes of others.

Anyway - past history, Dawn. Finito. La la la. End of story.

Interested in what you said about Delia Smith. "Not really a Channel 5 sort of person". Gotcha. Hear where you're coming from. You're saying Delia's really really sad, lacking in street cred, whereas Channel 5 is all about being sassy and in ya face.

Well - I think I've got something which will hit the G-spot, Dawn. Why do you think the circulation of the Independent on Sunday is going up? Because the editor, Rosie Boycott, although a wrinklie herself, is still half suss enough to have made it required reading for twentysomething must have, must do, airheads.

So that's the idea! 'MUST HAVE, MUST DO!' Style counselling for twentysomethings, fronted by a posh tart like Tara Palmer-Tompkinson or the Indie's own chic chick, Karen Krizanovitch. Karen's a babe but she isn't a bimbo.

Item 1. DON'T SAY YOU HAVEN'T: <u>Been to</u> . . . . a Wilde evening! Don't let Wilde mania pass you by! Oscar's grandson reads from his book on the quick-witted bard at 7pm on . . . . <u>Heard about</u> . . . . the new Muji, the extra large London store devoted to Japanese chic . . . . <u>Tried</u> . . . honey and garlic icecream at unique Swedish restaurant, Garlic and Shots . . .

Item 2. BRING BACK: . . . . . the Roller Disco! Yep. OK. Fine. Retro Eighties chic is here to stay! Want to choose a night life less ordinary? Bring back the roller disco!

Item 3. CIAO BABY!: . . . . . turn-ups! Strange things happen at the bottom of trouser-legs. This year's strides atrocity . . . . etc etc.
Does it do it for you, Dawn?
Ever

Liz Reed

Heart Felt Productions Limited

'A Tragedy Aired is a Tragedy Shared'

Tara Palmer-Tomkinson
c/o The Sunday Times
1 Pennington Street
London E1 9XW

Suites 139/140
Elm Park Mansions
Park Walk
LONDON
SW10 0AS

22nd October 1997

Tel: 0171-352-9689
Fax: 0171-376-8378

Dear Tara

MUST HAVE, MUST DO.

Hi there! Listen - we've just been commissioned by
Dawn Airey to pilot the above late-night style
counselling programme for Channel 5.

What we're looking for, yeah, are two or three
posh tarts with looks and attitude to act as
style gurus to what's in and what's you, where to
go and who to be seen with. It will be a weekly
guide for switched on, want-it-now mega-babes.

At the moment we're thinking you and we're thinking Karen Krizanovitch. Karen's a top lady. Bagsa
attitude and a bum to die for.

Hey - Karen's name literally spells 'now'!

Are you up for this one, honey?

Let me know!

Yours,

Liz

Liz Reed.

Directors: Jeff Boyd Liz Reed Martin Jacques
Simon King, Angela Picano (sicily)
Registered in England NO: 2905691

HEART FELT PRODUCTIONS

Suites 139-140
Elm Park Mansion
Park Walk
London SW10 0AS

Tel: 0171 352 9689
Fax: 0171 376 8378

Directors:
Steve Oboto
Ainsley Parrott
Winston Obogo
Simone Durity
P. Amin

Keith Hellawell
Drug Tzar!
c/o The Home Office
50 Queen Anne's Gate
London SW1H 9AT

16th October 1997

Dear Chief Constable

'<u>YOU'S BUSTED, MY MAN!</u>'

Congratulations from the brothers on your appointment as Drugs
Tzar. There's certainly a drug problem in this neighbourhood. You
can't get them!

Only jiving you, Chief Constable! In fact we're beaked up here
from soup to nuts. But we don't do crack, no man. Crack is <u>bad</u>.
Well, we do do crack, but only once or twice a week.

Word up, my man. This is the only independent production company
in the land run by the brothers. As our contribution to the Big
Drugs Debate we are piloting 'YOU'S BUSTED, MY MAN!' for Dawn
Airey at Channel 5 (and is <u>she</u> one mad honky chick!)

It wouldn't be shit if you appeared in this programme, Chief
Constable. The main man chilling out with the brothers, mixing
your funk with our funk.

You could cool out in front of the cameras while the brothers
did their shit with Bunsen burners and silver foil.

It would show the people that you intend to understand drugs at
street level.

Peace, my man.

Winston Obogo.

Chief Constable
Keith Hellawell, Q.P.M., L.B., M.Sc.

Assistant Chief Constable
(Designated Deputy)
Allan Charlesworth, q.p.m., f.i.mGT.

Assistant Chief Constables
Norman Bettison, M.A M.B.A.
D. Lloyd Clarke, M.A.
Paul T. Garvin, M.B.A., D.M.S., Dip. Crim., M.I.Mgt
Gregory Wilkinson, B.Sc., M.Inst.D.

Director of Finance
Jeffrey Goldthorpe, C.P.F.A.

WEST
YORKSHIRE
POLICE

POLICE HEADQUARTERS
P.O.Box 9, WAKEFIELD, WEST YORKSHIRE WF1 3QP
Teephone: Wakefield (01924)

Fax: (01924) 292180   **Telex: 517704(WYPOL)**

Our ref: CC/AEGB/MF   21 October 1997

Mr Winston Obogo
Heart Felt Productions Limited
Suites 139/140
Elm Park Mansions
Park Walk
LONDON SW10 0AS

Dear Mr Obogo

Thank you for inviting Chief Constable Mr Keith Hellawell to take part in a television programme regarding drugs. I can assure you that his knowledge of the issues is sufficient without having to appear on television with people who are actually taking drugs live on camera.

Thank you for your interest in this matter.

Yours sincerely

A E G Briggs BA (hons)
Chief Inspector
Staff Officer to Chief Constable

Heart Felt Productions Limited

'A Tragedy Aired is a Tragedy Shared'

The Managing Director
Hawkshead
46-47 Bedford Square
London WC1 3DP

22nd October 1997

Suites 139/140
Elm Park Mansions
Park Walk
LONDON
SW10 0AS
Tel: 0171-352-9689
Fax: 0171-376-8378

Dear Sir or Madam,

Hi there! We literally wrote to you on 11th October about Jane Root's new look for the BBC's cookery programmes.

We mentioned our close relationship with Dawn Airey (due to my mother having been at Girton with her) and suggested that we might be able to find Delia a slot at Channel 5.

Well! Things are moving faster than we expected! We have received a mega-excited letter from Dawn saying that Michael Attwell will take a meeting to discuss Delia's move!

I know what you're thinking. You're thinking, who in the name of arse is Michael Attwell?

Good question. And I've made it my business to find out the answer. He's Controller of Features and Arts at Channel 5.

So - do you and/or Delia want to bruise along to this meeting, or would you prefer for us to carry out the initial spade-work (or should I say spatula work!)

Hey - be nice!

Yours,

Liz

Liz Reed.

Directors: Jeff Boyd Liz Reed Martin Jacques
Simon King, Angela Picano (Sicily)
Registered in England NO: 2905691

BAZAL

Liz Reed
Heart Felt Productions Ltd

Nov 14th 97

Dear Liz,

I am fortunate to have had your letter passed to me — dated 22nd October and addressed to the Managing-Director of Hushhead. Fortunate? Yes, because rarely have I read such a compassionate piece of prose. Your concern for Delia Smith has shown me that there is good in the world after all.

Whether a cook, writer and T.V. Presenter of Delia's emminence would want to have anything to do with your obscure outfit is hard to say. But you seem to have an 'in' with Denon Airey. The Girton connection would prove decisive. It was certainly decisive in my days at Cambridge — such a long bicycle ride from the centre of town for sex. By the time I got there I never seemed up to it, so to speak. But there you are. Oh, by the way,

46/47 Bedford Square, London WC1B 3DP Telephone: +44 171 462 9462 Facsimile: +44 171 462 9998

if it's relevant, we no longer produce Delia. Toodle Pip. Yours BAZ.

Broadcast Communications plc trading as Bazal Productions Ltd
REGISTERED IN ENGLAND 1692513
REGISTERED OFFICE: 46/47 BEDFORD SQUARE, LONDON WC1B 3DP
VAT REGISTERED: 466 5371 14

Dawn Airey
Director of Programmes

3rd November 1997

Liz Reed
Heart Felt Productions Limited
Suites 139/140
Elm Park Mansions
Park Walk
London. SW10 0AS

Dear Liz,

I am sorry to have to inform you but I think somebody has stolen a quantity of your letter-headed paper and is sending me in your name a bunch of ill-conceived proposals.

May I suggest that you find out who is responsible for this act and stop it immediately.

Yours sincerely,

Dawn Airey

c.c. Michael Attwell, w/encs.

Channel 5 Broadcasting Limited 22 Long Acre London WC23 9LY
Telephone : 0171 550 5555 Faxcimile: 0171 550 5554

Registered in England no: 3147460

Studio B 11 Edith Grove Chelsea London SW10 0JZ Telephone 0171-823 3723 fax 0171-351 3711

Liz Reed
Heart Felt Productions Limited
Elm Park Mansions
Park Walk
London
SW10 0AS

Friday 21 November 1997

Dear Liz,

Thank you for your letter dated 22nd October and 14th
November 1997 concerning your interest in Tara Palmer-
Tomkinson as a possible style guru for your new programme.
We did try and get in touch with you to discuss this venture fur-
ther but unfortunately we were unable to reach you.

Tara's diary is now getting very booked up but do please get in
touch with us and we can see if we are able to work together.
Once again thank you for your interest.

Yours sincerely

Martine Montgomery

Heart Felt Productions Limited

'A Tragedy Aired is a Tragedy Shared'

David Liddiment
ITV Network Centre
200 Gray's Inn Road
London WC1X 8HF

Suites 139/140
Elm Park Mansions
Park Walk
LONDON
SW10 0AS

24th October 1997

Tel: 0171-352-9689
Fax: 0171-376-8378

Dear David

Here at Heart Felt we have two proposals which we would like to pitch to the Network at this time.

1. 'DISABLED GLADIATORS!'

Our two presenters – Pru Stokes and legless Falklands hero, Bob 'Jumper' Cross – and our disabled contestants will appear under their real names.

Our Disabled Gladiators, on the other hand, will be given appropriate stage names, as follows:

Mad Cow, Thrush, Prozac, Parkinson, Alzheimer, Huntingdon, Delirium Tremens, Tourettes Syndrome etc.

Thus:

"Disabled contestant! You will go on my first whistle!"

"Irritable Bowel Syndrome! You will go on my second whistle!"

The venue for the games must, obviously, have special back-stage facilities – levels, inclines etc – easily negotiated by folk in traction.

Plus, one of our contracted Gladiators – Pip the Mighty Squeak – has a special disability. He is only 2ft 3ins tall. It is important that there is at least one shower-head in the Gladiators' changing-room which is only 30 inches off the floor.

A regular shower-head blows Pip the Mighty Squeak all

over the tub.

Please check on this before progressing the proposal, David.

2. 'JANE'S PHOTO-FILE.'

Originally an item in our development 'WHO PUT HEROIN IN MY KIDDIES' SWEETS?' - and a casualty of Birt's dumbing down policies at the BBC - this was to have been a dramatised version of Jane Butterworth's celebrated column in The News of the World.

Personable young Equity members would have acted out problems of the sort submitted to Agony Aunts, and Jane herself would have been present in the studio to offer her advice.

We believe that this - presented by someone with early evening cred (Cilla, perhaps, or Dale) rather than the Butterworth woman - would make a valid programme on its own.

As I read the situation, there's no need at the moment to tell Butterworth that we're dropping her - nor that we are having her scripts rewritten to a professional standard. I now enclose a selection of these, together with copies of Butterworth's originals.

Enjoy!

Yours,

Liz

Liz Reed.

enc. 'JANE'S PHOTO-FILE'. (Professional rewrites).

Directors: Jeff Boyd Liz Reed Martin Jacques
Simon King, Angela Picano (Sicily)
Registered in England NO: 2905691

Heart Felt Productions Limited

'STILL ON FILE WITH RADIO 4! YEAH!'

Caroline Elliot
BBC Radio 4
Broadcasting House
London W1A 1AA

Suites 139/140
Elm Park Mansions
Park Walk
LONDON
SW10 0AS

26th October 1997

Tel: 0171-352-9689
Fax: 0171-376-8378

Dear Caroline,

Thanks for yours of 24th October, and for the enclosed questionnaire.

Don't worry! We haven't forgotten you here at Heart Felt in spite of our many commitments. In fact, I was talking about you only yesterday to my colleague Jeff, and the problems our development 'WITH FRIENDS LIKE THIS . . . .' is causing us.

Did I say problems? Well, <u>that's</u> the understatement of the century! We must have written to literally thousands of celebs and so far not <u>one</u> of them has agreed to put in a word for Jeremy Isaacs.

You'd think we were asking people to speak up for Rick Stein or Janet Street-Porter. I mean, it's <u>weird</u>.

We won't give up, though, Caroline, and I promise to return the questionnaire thingy before 7th November. Hey - it looks like a lotta fun.

All the best.

Yours,

Liz

Liz Reed.

Directors: Jeff Boyd Liz Reed Martin Jacques
Simon King, Angela Picano (Sicily)
Registered in England NO: 2905691

Heart Felt Productions Limited

` A tragedy Aired is a Tragedy Shared'

Kevin Lygo
Channel 4
124 Horseferry Road
London SW1P 2TX

23rd October 1997

Suites 139/140
Elm Park Mansions
Park Walk
LONDON
SW10 0AS
Tel: 0171-352-9689
Fax: 0171-376-8378

Dear Kevin

`BACK TO SQUARE ONE!'

This will blow your skirt up, Kevin! Here's the take:
various fat top types who have made mega-pillocks of
themselves (through lust, greed, vanity or whatever) are
lured to the studios to take part (they think!) in `MY
SIDE OF THE STORY!' - a rehab docu which will restore
their reputations.
Imagine it, Kevin: in the Green Room - their smooth piggy
pink faces aglow with hospitality and misplaced confidence
- Major `Ron' Ferguson, Jeffrey Archer, Cecil Parkinson,
Norman Tebbit, Jerry Hayes, David Mellor, Neil Hamilton,
Alan Clark, Jonathan Aitken, Norman Lamont, Frank Bough,
Piers Merchant, Ian Hislop . . . . . .

"We're laughing," they think. "We've done our porridge."

Well, bums to them! They've been set up like skittles in
a bowling alley!

Behind the scenes, scraggy people from their pasts are
ready to run on and spoil the party!

Common girls in riot skirts and bondage boots, nasty little rent boys, dealers, dominatrixes, Anna Cox, Mona
Bauwens, Lady Bienvenida Buck, Monica Coghlan, Antonia de
Sancha, Fat Pat, Dopey Linda, Kenneth Noye, Max Clifford,
foul-mouthed Muslims clutching envelopes . . .

Hilarious or what, Kevin? Is the Pope a Catholic?

We're ready to pilot - so whaddya say?

Have a great one!

Yours,

Liz

Liz Reed.

Directors: Jeff Boyd Liz Reed Martin Jacques
Simon King, Angela Picano (Sicily)
Registered in England NO: 2905691

Heart Felt Productions Limited

'A Tragedy Aired is A Tragedy Shared'

The Managing Director
The Charter Clinic
Radnor Walk
London SW3

Suites 139/140
Elm Park Mansions
Park Walk
LONDON
SW10 0AS

6th November 1997

Tel: 0171 352 968
Fax: 0171 376 8378

Dear Sir or Madam

Can you cure Tourettes Syndrome? One of our directors, Liz Reed, seems to be suffering from this distressing condition. An alternative diagnosis might be that her hormones are out of control due to testosterone overload.

Her behaviour is becoming a business liability, the symptoms involving a volley of obscenities directed at anyone who thwarts her in the least.

This is a bi-media communications outfit, progressing family product across a range of Triumph over Tragedy subjects. If a member of the general public is blown up in an outrage or a grieving mother has a tot with a diaphragmatic hernia we ask them to talk about it in an early evening slot.

Our cause is not helped when a mad woman or major player is told to "Get bent!" by e-mail or, if Liz has their number, down their mobile phone.

Last week a man who does state occasions and royal funerals for the BBC was in a meeting with the Director General. Liz rang his mobile number and called him a tub of monkey poo.

This is no laughing matter. Can you help?

We have asked Liz to seek professional advice, or at least to take a holiday, but these well-meant suggestions have been met with a volley of fresh abuse.

I look forward to hearing from you.

Yours sincerely

Jeff Boyd.

Directors: Jeff Boyd Liz Reed Martin Jacques
Simon King, Angela Picano (Sicily)
Registered in England NO: 2905691

Charter Nightingale Hospital

26th November 1997

11-19 Lisson Grove
London NW1 6SH
Telephone: 0171-258 3828
Facsimile: 0171-724 8294

Mr Boyd
Heart Felt Productions Ltd
Suites 139/140
Elm Park Mansions
Park Walk
London
SW10   0AS

Dear Mr Boyd

Thank you for your letter regarding outpatient services at Charter Hospitals London.

At present we have two outpatient departments in Central London. One is based in the Chelsea area and the other in the Marylebone area.

We are able to treat a wide range of disorders and can offer flexible appointment times.

Please find enclosed a profile of Consultants and Therapists which can be accessed through our 24 hour Helpline on 0171 258 3828.

Yours sincerely

Zsara Hodgkinson
Community Liaison Manager

Charter Medical of England Ltd , No. 1431836. Registered in England, 1-5 Radnor Walk, London SW3 4BP

CHANNEL FOUR TELEVISION   124 HORSEFERRY ROAD,LONDON SWIP 2TX
TELEPHONE: 0171-396-4444.DIRECT LINE:0171-306 8700
FAX: 0171-306 8356.
MINICOM: 0171-306 8691
EMAIL: CLANGDON@CHANNEL4.CO.UK

Our Ref: CL/EF/7102907

31 October 1997

Liz Reed
Heart Felt Productions Limited
Suites 139/140
Elm Park Mansions
Park Walk
London SW10 0AS

Dear Liz

Thank you for sending in the proposal for 'Back to Square One', which Kevin Lygo
passed on to me.

It's certainly an ambitious project! However, having broadcast Chris Morris's "Brass
Eye" earlier this year, and with Mark Thomas's second series about to go into production, I don't feel that the time is right to embark upon an idea which, although not
identical, covers some of the same ground as these two shows.

I'm sorry not to be more positive, but thanks again for contacting us, and good luck
with 'Heart Felt Productions'.

Yours sincerely

Caroline Leddy
Commissioning Editor
Entertainment

CHANNEL FOUR TELEVISION
SIR MICHAEL BISHOP CBE(CHAIRMAN), DAVID PLOWRIGHT(DEPUTY CHAIRMAN)
MICHAEL JACKSON(CHIEF EXECUTIVE), STEWART BUTTERFIELD (DIRECTOR ADVERTISING SALES AND MARKETING), COLIN LEVENTHAL
(DIRECTOR OF ACQUISITION).
FRANK McGETTIGAN (DIRECTOR AND GENERAL MANAGER), DAVID SCOTT (MANAGING DIRECTOR), JOHN WILLIS(DIRECTOR OF PROGRAMMES).
SECRETARY: ANDREW YEATES

31st October 1997

Liz Reed
Heart Felt Productions Limited
Suites 139/140
Elm Park Mansions
Park Walk
LONDON SW10 0AS

Macmillan General Books

25 Eccleston Place
London
SW1W 9NF

Tel: 0171 881 8000
Fax: 0171 881 8001

Dear Liz

Thanks for sending me Amy Jenkins' screenplay, IS THIS
ALLOWED? I shared it with a couple of colleagues here
but I'm afraid we don't feel able to commit to anything at this early stage.
We're currently re-assessing our tie-in publishing and would feel happier con-
templating a novelisation once the film has been made.

We found the characterisation strong and very much enjoyed the opening
scenes but I have to confess that we were a little disappointed with the ending. Perhaps, once filmed, we'll be able to see more clearly how the script ties
together.

I'd be grateful if you'd continue to bear us in mind during filming but, as
above, we simply don't feel we can progress this project for the time being.

Very many thanks for sharing the screenplay with us.
With best wishes
Yours

Mari Evans

Encs

A Division Of Macmillan Publishers Ltd.

Registered Office:
Brunel Road
Houndmills
Basingstoke
Hampshire RG21 6XS

Registered Number: 758998 England

Heart Felt Productions Limited

'A Tragedy Aired is a Tragedy Shared'

Mari Evans
Macmillan
25 Eccleston Place
London SW1W 9NF

Suites 139/140
Elm Park Mansions
Park Walk
LONDON
SW10 0AS

7th November 1997

Tel: 0171-352-9689
Fax: 0171-376-8378

Dear Mari,

Well! Thanks a whole <u>lot</u>!

I mean, hey, my life's just hit an all time fucking
low, my same sex partner's gone off with my drug dealer, I haven't had a holiday in six weeks and what do I
get?

I get your really <u>bloody</u> unhelpful response to Amy
Jenkins's original screenplay, IS THIS ALLOWED?

I mean, for Christ's sake, Mari, Amy <u>toils</u> away for a
year doing <u>countless</u> rewrites (each supervised, I may
say, by Danny Boyle) and then you come along and say
the ending's no bloody good!

I mean, what in the name of arse is going on? Do you
suddenly know more than Danny Boyle or something?

Who asked you anyway? What the hell do you know about
films?

Might I suggest you stick to publishing books, and
only give your opinion of an original screenplay when
it's asked for?

Thanks <u>again</u>.

Yours,

Liz

Liz Reed.

Directors: Jeff Boyd Liz Reed Martin Jacques
Simon King, Angela Picano (Sicily)
Registered in England NO: 2905691

Heart Felt Productions Limited

'A Tragedy Aired is a Tragedy Shared'

Jane Butterworth
The News of the World
1 Virginia Street
London E1 9XR

Suites 139/140
Elm Park Mansions
Park Walk
LONDON
SW10 0AS

31st October 1997

Tel: 0171-352-9689
Fax: 0171-376-8378

Dear Jane

'<u>WHO PUT HEROIN IN MY KIDDIES' SWEETS?</u>'

Hey - <u>really</u> sorry I've taken such an age to get back to you. I've had a couple of problems. Nothing too horrendous. Girls' stuff really. A row with my personal trainer and the decorators have made a horlicks of my new bathroom.

Oh - and the BBC have dropped 'WHO PUT HEROIN IN MY KIDDIES' SWEETS?'

Not really your fault.

And the good news is that we're now dealing with David Liddiment at the ITV Network Centre.

Plus, we hired some professional writers to give your scripts a sharper edge. I think you'll be chuffed with their improvements, which I now enclose.

I've sent these off to David Liddiment at the Network Centre, and will pass his comments on to you as soon as I get them.

All the best, Jane.

Yours,

Liz

Liz Reed.

Directors: Jeff Boyd Liz Reed Martin Jacques
Simon King, Angela Picano (Sicily)
Registered in England NO: 2905691

BY FAX

Liz Reed
Heart Felt Productions Ltd
Suites 139/140
Elm Park Mansions
Park Walk
London SW10 0AS

24 November 1997

We seem to have been talking at cross purposes. I was under the impression that you had been commissioned by the BBC to actually make this pilot, and that they had agreed and approved the format – I did not realise you were still touting the idea around. Furthermore, your colleague, to whom I spoke on the phone, led me to believe that the tone of this programme was *ironic*. That was why I expressed an interest in knowing more.

However, after having read the scripts you sent me it seems I have been under a misapprehension. I like to think that the humour in my picture stories is subtle and even witty. The scripts you sent me are neither. They are crass, infantile, sneering and devoid of humour and I cannot believe you are naive enough to think you could say words such as 'cunt' or even 'fuck' on prime time television.

An agony column treads a fine line between entertainment and helping people. As well as editing my page each week, I reply personally to all the hundreds of letters I receive – many of which are written by very distressed and troubled people. Do you really think I could go on television and ridicule these people? Because that is what you are suggesting I do.

Apart from the fact that the News of the World would not countenance me appearing on such a programme, if I did such a thing I would destroy the trust of my readers. I doubt if anyone would ever write to me again, which would make my job difficult indeed as an agony page is totally dependent on the letters it receives.

I am also very concerned that you sent these 'revised' scripts without my permission to David Liddiment. I hope you made it quite clear that I was not responsible for writing them, and I would like you to confirm this to me in writing.

Had I been able to talk to you and you had made it clear from the outset what sort of programme you were planning, I would have told you there and then that there is no way I could be associated with such a project.

Yours sincerely

JANE BUTTERWORTH

Heart Felt Productions Limited

'A Tragedy Aired is a Tragedy Shared'

Jane Butterworth

FAX NO: 01432 840 866

24th November 1997

Suites 139/140
Elm Park Mansions
Park Walk
LONDON
SW10 0AS
Tel: 0171-352-9689
Fax: 0171-376-8378

Dear Jane,

Oh dear. Your fax of today's date really upset me - but I shall try to keep calm.

Would you not accept, Jane, that we, being professionals, are better judges of a TV script's viability than you? As is well-known, it's extremely difficult for someone who is not in the business to know whether a sketch will, as we say, "play".

All I can tell you is that David Liddiment is as excited by this concept as we are and it would be extremely detrimental to the project to tell him now that you have reservations about the scripts.

I suppose we could ask him to take your name off the credits, but I think he might, in these circumstances, cancel the whole programme. In which case, we might, of course, have to look to you for compensation.

I really hope you'll take a deep breath, Jane, and re-read the scripts. If you do, I think you'll begin to see how closely they stick to your originals.

Meanwhile, we are trying them out at the end of next week with some artistes from Samantha Bond and Yvonne Paul. Do you know the Page 3 Scorchers, Jo Guest and Rachel Garley? We think they will be terrific as the girls.

Perhaps you'd like to come to these rehearsals? Seeing your work performed by professionals might make you see how greatly our writers have improved it.
Let me know.
All the best.

Yours,

Liz

Liz Reed.

Directors: Jeff Boyd Liz Reed Martin Jacques
Simon King, Angela Picano (Sicily)
Registered in England NO: 2905691

NEWS OF THE WORLD

THE WORLDS LARGEST SUNDAY SALE

1 VIRGINIA STREET, LONDON, E1 9XR
Telephone: 0171-782 1000
Fax: 0171-583 9504

Liz Reed
Heart Felt Productions Ltd
Suites 139/140
Elm Park Mansions
Park Walk
London SW10 0AS

28 November

Dear Liz

I am sorry you were upset by my fax – but believe me,
I was pretty upset when I was confronted by the *fait
accomplis* of having my picture story scripts rewritten.

When I first wrote to you on the 15 September indicat-
ing interest, I said it was '*subject to the News of
the World's approval.*' The News of the World allow me
to do TV appearances on the understanding that I appear
as their agony aunt, and they have to approve any
appearances I make which involve the giving off advice.
When I left a message for you to call me some weeks
back it was because I had spoken to the Managing
Editor for the News of the World and he had certain
reservations about your project, which I wanted to discuss with you. You didn't get back to me, so I assumed
the whole thing had been dropped.

I have not signed a contract with you, nor agreed a
fee. I have done nothing, in fact, except register my
interest in principle for a project about which I have
received only the sketchiest of details – and which
initially, I was told was a BBC commission.

When I told you I wanted to write the new scripts
myself, it was partly because it would avoid hassle
with the NOTW but also because I wanted to retain some
degree of autonomy. Your reply was to invite me to
write you a specimen script. Again, I left a message
on your answering machine asking you to call me as I
wanted to discuss this with you. You didn't – so I put
it to the back of my already overcrowded mind.

Then out of the blue I receive a letter from you

telling me you have had my picture story scripts rewritten
by someone without so much of a by your leave. Furthermore,
you have sent them to David Liddiment without asking my permission. I was flabbergasted. Can I remind you that the
copyright for this material belongs to the News of the
World? And that you are infringing that copyright if you
broadcast them without their permission? I think if anyone
will be seeking compensation it will be the News of the
World.

TEXT OBSCURE . . . caring, sympathetic, responsible, etc,
etc, simply isn't so.

I spoke to your colleague on the phone back in September
and asked him if this was intended as a piss take. Oh no,
he replied, it will be similar to your column, and if there
is humour it will be ironic.

Your fax of 1 October said, 'With regard to the problems.
(that would be featured in the programme). The choice should
be yours. They should be serious, but this does not mean
that they can't contain an element of humour, even wit. But
they should be sensitive and helpful . . .'

I felt reassured when I read this but if these scripts are
an example of what you plan, this is clearly not the case.
Furthermore, you seem to want me to go on air and give
someone else's advice, not mine, as the rewritten advice
bears no resemblance to my original. You have, in effect,
moved the goalposts - and if that's the case, I don't want
to play.

If only you had phoned me back after I had left messages on
your answering machine weeks ago we would both be clear
about what we meant and there would be no misunderstandings.
I am not against this project, but if I am to take part in
it it must be on my terms. If you think we have anything
more we can usefully say on the matter, please give me a
call.

Yours sincerely

JANE BUTTERWORTH

Registered Office: News Group NewspapersLtd., P.O.Box495, Virginia Street, London E1 9XY
Registered No: 679251 England

Heart Felt Productions Limited

'A Tragedy Aired is a Tragedy Shared'

Jane Butterworth

FAX NO: 01432 840 866

2nd December 1997

Suites 139/140
Elm Park Mansions
Park Walk
LONDON
SW10 0AS

Tel: 0171-352-9689
Fax: 0171-376-8378

Dear Jane,

Hey - what can I do other than repeat my position of 24th November? In any case, things have moved on since then - and it's impossible to call a halt once a production's under way (as you'd know yourself if you'd ever worked in TV). It's just too late now to cancel everything on the whim of just _one_ of the contributors.

I can think of only two solutions:

1. We go to arbitration, getting an expert ruling from a panel of industry professionals - Debbie Mason, Geoff Atkinson, Mark Chapman or Pete 'The Schnoz' Morgan, say - as to which version of the scripts is better, yours or the ones done by professionals.

2. We broadcast some sort of disclaimer at the end of the show. Something along the lines, perhaps:

'Miss Jane Butterworth, the author of 'Jane's Photo-File', wishes it to be known that the improvements made to her scripts were not done by her.'

I dare say this could be done - _if_ David Liddiment agrees. However, I'm sure he'd want you to bear the costs.

Let me have your reaction to these suggestions.

Very best wishes.

Yours,

Liz Reed.

Directors: Jeff Boyd Liz Reed Martin Jacques
Simon King, Angela Picano (Sicily)
Registered in England NO: 2905691

NEWS OF THE **WORLD**

THE WORLDS LARGEST SUNDAY SALE

1 VIRGINIA STREET, LONDON, E1 9XR
Telephone: 0171-782 1000
Fax: 0171-583 9504

TO: Liz Reed, fax no 0171-376 8378

FROM: Jane Butterworth

Dear Liz –

As my telephone messages seem destined to remain unanswered, I'll try the fax.

<u>PLEASE</u> could you call me ASAP.

We need to talk!!

Registered Office: News Group NewspapersLtd., P.O.Box495, Virginia Street, London E1 9XY
Registered No: 679251 England

KARL MARX

Geoff Loynes

CHARLIE CHAPLIN

Lawrence Simmons

Heart Felt Productions Limited

'A Tragedy Aired is a Tragedy Shared'

Karen Black   Suites 139/140
LOOK-ALIKES   Elm Park Mansions
13 Cinnamon Row   Park Walk
Plantation Wharf   LONDON
London SW11 3TW   SW10 0AS

6th November 1997   Tel: 0171-352-9689
                                Fax: 0171-376-8378

Dear Karen

'<u>LEST WE FORGET</u>.'

Good talking to you on the blower. Yeah, £600 for
Christina is certainly within the ball-park. All of
us here at Heart Felt look forward to working with
her.

Hey - thanks too for sending me more look-alikes.
Karl Marx and Charlie Chaplin are two of your best
so far! Now on file with Heart Felt!

Hey - you could add that to their CV's! 'Karl Marx
- Now on File with Heart Felt!' 'Charlie Chaplin -
Now on File with Heart Felt!'

Send us a contract for Christina soonest.

See ya!

Liz

Liz Reed.

Directors: Jeff Boyd Liz Reed Martin Jacques
Simon King, Angela Picano (Sicily)
Registered in England NO: 2905691

FAX MESSAGE FROM
LOOK ALIKES

13 Cinnamon Row
Plantation Whaf
London SW11 3TV
Fax No: +44 171-924 2662
Phone: +44 171-924 4447

DATE: November 1997
NO OF PAGES: Two
SENT TO: Liz Reed
MESSAGE FROM: Karen Black

Hi Liz

Thank you for your letter dated 6 November 1997.

Please accept the following contract as a confirmation that we agree
to the £600 fee for Christina Hance to appear on your Christmas
video.

Please can you check through the contract, sign and fax it back to me
when you get a chance. A top copy is in the post to you today.

Regards

Karen Black

Karen Black

Heart Felt Productions Limited

'A Tragedy Aired is a Tragedy Shared'

The Senior Legal Manager
The BBC
Broadcasting House
London W1A 1AA

Suites 139/140
Elm Park Mansions
Park Walk
LONDON
SW10 0AS

7th November 1997

Tel: 0171-352-9689
Fax: 0171-376-8378

Dear Sir or Madam

We have noticed that in the last few weeks the show entitled
'ESTHER' on BBC2 no longer features a performer of that
name, least of all Ms Esther Rantzen. Instead, alternating
hawk-faced women in trouser-suits appear in her place.

This suggests to us that 'ESTHER' is now a concept or 'formula' with no guarantee what Ms Rantzen will be appearing in
it.

If we are correct in this assumption, does it follow that
the BBC has been able to establish a copyright in this formula, or would it be possible for an independent programme-
maker to produce and market a show called 'ESTHER'?

Alternatively, if the BBC has managed to establish copyright, does it intend to franchise this formula (disturbed
women quizzed in a confessional atmosphere) to sub-contrac-
tors for royalties or a down-payment?

I can think of many businesses which have franchised themselves successfully. MacDonalds. Kall Kwik. Rymans. Hobby
Lobby. Bolloms the same day cleaners. That's to name only a
few.

'ESTHER' should do the same!

I look forward to hearing from you.

Yours sincerely,

Jeff Boyd.

B B C Production

Legal Affairs Section
Commercial and Buisness Affairs

14 November 1997

Mr J Boyd
Heart Felt Productions Limited
Suites 139/140
Elm Park Mansions
Park Walk
London SW10 0AS

Dear Mr Boyd,

Thank you for your letter of 7th November 1997.

In reply to your first question, Esther Rantzen is scheduled to return to the show as presenter in January next year.

It is difficult to see the commercial logic in there being two different shows with identical names as this would certainly detract from the BBC's good will in its show. For the record I should state that the BBC would strongly resist any attempts by a third party to produce a programme derived from the BBC's programme. The BBC asserts exclusive rights in its programmes "Esther" both in the UK and worldwide and does not wish to license rights in it in the manner you suggest.

Yours sincerely,

David Hudson
Senior Lawyer
Legal Affairs
Commercial & Business Affairs
BBC Production

Heart Felt Productions Limited

'A Tragedy Aired is a Tragedy Shared'

The Rt Hon Tony Blair
10 Downing Street
London SW1

Suites 139/140
Elm Park Mansions
Park Walk
LONDON
SW10 0AS

10th November 1997

Tel: 0171-352-9689
Fax: 0171-376-8378

Dear Tony

<u>'LEST WE FORGET!'</u>

Hi there! It's me again! have you finalised plans yet for a Christmas compassion initiative?

If not, this could be half a chance: in association with the Dean of St Paul's, we have nearly completed a charity video in memory of Diana, Princess of Wales.

We've got the Dean, Chris de Burgh, Mr Motivator, Lord Deedes, Wayne Sleep, Billy Connolly, Kriss Akabussi, Clive James, Michael Barrymore (the troubled funnyman) and Christina Hance, the celebrated Diana look-alike.

What we don't have at the moment is someone who is currently 'bankable' to top the bill. So here's what we did: we commissioned MediaLab to research who's 'hot' right now and to report back to us.

Well! You 'researched' sixth best, Tony! Equal first were TV Glamour babes Carol Smillie and Carol Vorderman. Then came Anthea Turner, Gaby Roslin and Fern Britton! (Seventh was Ainsley Harriott and eight was Zoe Ball.)

Anyway, the two Carols are literally tied up for months, as are Anthea, Fern and Gaby – so that leaves you to top the bill, Tony! Will you do it for us (and for Diana, too, of course)?

And, hey, could you fill in the enclosed 'Fave Things' Questionnaire?? It's for our PR people. Ta!

Cool Britannia! Yeah! Yeah! Yeah!
Yours,

Liz

Liz Reed.

Directors: Jeff Boyd Liz Reed Martin Jacques
Simon King, Angela Picano (Sicily)
Registered in England NO: 2905691

HEART FELT PRODUCTIONS.
PUBLICITY DEPARTMENT.

Kindly complete your answers in space provided and return.

1. What's your most glam feature?

2. Can you itemise the contents of your handbag, and are they essential?

3. How much do you spend per week on beauty products?

4. What's your fave song to sing on Karaoke Night?

5. Do you think you're sexy?

6. How often do you think about sex?

7. Who was the last person you snogged?

8. Have you ever snogged Chris Evans?

9. Have you ever been sick in the back of a taxi?

10. Have you ever presented 'Top of the Pops' without wearing knickers?

Heart Felt Productions Limited

'A Tragedy Aired is a Tragedy Shared'

The Rt Hon Tony Blair
10 Downing Street
London SW1.

Suites 139/140
Elm Park Mansions
Park Walk
LONDON
SW10 0AS

12th November 1997

Tel: 0171-352-9689
Fax: 0171-376-8378

Dear Tony

'<u>LEST WE FORGET!</u>'

Sorreee! Our really crap PR department sent you the wrong Questionnaire!

They must have thought you were in another of our developments - 'LIPPY CHICKS', for Dawn Airey at Channel 5. This will feature 'Top Of The Pops' babes Zoe Ball, Jayne Middlemiss and Jo Whiley and the idea is to find out whether they're as loud, leery and lusty as the lads!

Fun, yeah?

Anyway, I now enclose the Questionnaire they should have sent you. Could you fill it in and return as soon as poss? Ta.

Yours,

Liz

Liz Reed.

Directors: Jeff Boyd Liz Reed Martin Jacques
Simon King, Angela Picano (Sicily)
Registered in England NO: 2905691

HEART FELT PRODUCTIONS.   PUBLICITY DEPARTMENT.

Kindly complete your answers in space provided and return.

1.   Fave band?

2.   Fave movie moment?

3.   Fave movie kiss?

4.   Fave car?

5.   Fave character in a TV soap?

6.   Fave colleague?

7.   Least fave colleague?

8.   Colleague with most crap haircut?

9.   Worst dressed colleague?

10.   Fave club?

11.   Most embarrassing moment in a club!?!?

12.   Fave job for 'Ginger' Spice when it all goes pear-shaped?

    (a)   Masseuse in West London Sauna Parlour?

    (b)   Check-out girl at Birmingham branch of Safeways?

    (c)   Air hostess for Dan Air?

    (d)   Editor of the Daily Express?

10 DOWNING STREET
LONDON SW1A 2AA

21 November 1997

Dear Ms Reed

The Prime Minister has asked me to thank you for your letter of 10 November asking him to take part in a video tribute to the Princess of Wales.

Unfortunately, his diary commitments at the moment make it impossible for him to accept your invitation.

I am sorry to send you a disappointing reply.
Yours sincerely

Yours sincerely

HILARY COFFMAN
Press Office

Ms Liz Reed
Heart Felt Productions Limited

Heart Felt Productions Limited

'A Tragedy Aired is a Tragedy Shared'

Michael Winner
The News of the World
1 Virginia Street
London E1 9XR

10th November 1997

Dear Michael

Suites 139/140
Elm Park Mansions
Park Walk
LONDON
SW10 0AS
Tel: 0171-352-9689
Fax: 0171-376-8378

'LEST WE FORGET!'

Hey - <u>love</u> your column in the News of the World. Some of your one-liners are as good as Ingrid Miller's. Here's one of yours from last week.

'If William Hague is a marvellous orator Frank Bruno is a nuclear physicist!'

I've often wondered - do one-liners like that just come to you, or do you really have to work at it?

On a more serious note, Michael - have you finalised your plans yet for a Christmas compassion initiative - yourself with a floral tribute, perhaps, at the grave of WPC Nona Mackay?

If you have nothing definite in the pipeline yet might I suggest that you join the cast of our musical tribute to Diana Princess of Wales? So far we have booked the Dean of St Paul's, Chris de Burgh, Wayne Sleep, Lionel Blair, Christopher Biggins, Michael Barrymore (the troubled comedian), Christina Hance - the celebrated Diana look-alike - and the grieving parents of Leah Betts.

What we lack at the moment is a big finish, and this is where you might be able to help us, Michael. We want someone with marquee value in the compassion business and reckon it's between you, Esther Rantzen and the Prime Minister. Alas, Esther is unwell, and, while we have approached the Prime Minister, we rather fear he may be too busy.

So - will you be our Top Banana, Michael?

Let us know soonest. We have to be in the can by 6th Dec at the latest.

Break a leg!
Yours,

Liz

Liz Reed.

Directors: Jeff Boyd Liz Reed Martin Jacques
Simon King, Angela Picano (Sicily)
Registered in England NO: 2905691

*Thank you so much for writing.
I really do appreciate it. It
was very interesting to read what
you had to say.*

Good luck and God bless.

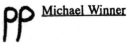

PP <u>Michael Winner</u>

1 Virginia Street, London E1 9BD

Heart Felt Productions Limited

'A Tragedy Aired is a Tragedy Shared'

Mrs Anita Butt
The Deanery
9 Amen Corner
London EC4 7BU

11th November 1997

Suites 139/140
Elm Park Mansions
Park Walk
LONDON
SW10 0AS
Tel: 0171 352 9689
Fax: 0171 376 8378

Dear Mrs Butt

'DI-SGUSTING!'

We have now completed principal photography on our
Christmas compassion video, save for the Dean's contribution.

However, we have run into a small problem. It turns out
that our star artiste - Miss Christina Hance - is a tart
and a drug fiend. She has been exposed as such in the
News of the World. A rival compassion company has drawn
this to our attention. ('DI-SGUSTING!' - cutting
enclosed).

I know what you're thinking, Mrs Butt. You're thinking,
so what? And I agree with you. We all have private lives,
and it has never been a condition of their employment
that our artistes first assure us in writing that they
are neither tarts nor drug friends.

For this and other reasons I am perfectly happy to be
associated with Miss Hance, and I am sure the Dean will
feel the same.

Motes and beams, camels and haystacks, eyes and needles,
first stones etc.

That said, I thought it best to warn you that there might
be a certain amount of negative publicity when the video
is released.

If you could confirm that the Dean is still happy to per-
form the opening number I'll send you what we have in the
can by return.
Ta!
Yours,

Liz
Liz Reed.

Directors: Jeff Boyd Liz Reed Martin Jacques
Simon King, Angela Picano (Sicily)
Registered in England NO: 2905691

Liz Reed
Heart Felt Productions Ltd.
Suites 139/140
Elm Park Mansions
London
SW10 0AS
13/11/97

Dear Liz,

We are currently in preproduction on a Channel 4 documentary, focusing on 3 Princess Diana look-a-likes. One of these women is Christina Hance who we understand is due to appear in Chris de Burgh's video "There's a new Star in Heaven Tonight" as part of the Princess Diana Tribute video. Our documentary will be following the careers of these three women, what kind of impact the Princess' life and death has had on their lives, and how they have contributed to the making of one of the 20th century's most powerful icons.

We would be particularly keen to film Christina's participation in your music video, as it must be the most important and serious appearance of her career, and as such very important to our study of her life. Christina is very keen that we be able to include this in our programme.

Of course we understand your filming logistics and pressures and as a small documentary crew of 4, would cause as little disturbance as possible. We would be able to fit around your schedules.

Please contact me if you want any further details about our production. I look forward to hearing from you, and hope very much that we will be able to film with you.

With best wishes

Polly Nash
Production Manager

BRIGHT PICTURES
Televis
and   Fi
Product
Eurolink   Ce
49   Effra
London   SW2
Tel: 0171   738
Fax: 0171   738

Email: info@brighter-pictures.co.uk
Associate Office: 8205 Santica Monica Boulevard Suite 1427 Los Angeles California 90046-5967 Te: 213 960 5034
Reg. In England & Wales No:2597 443. Registered OfficeFiveChanceryLang Cliffords Inn London EC4A 1GU NO. 60789885

Heart Felt Productions Limited

'A Tragedy Aired is a Tragedy Shared'

Polly Nash
Brighter Pictures
Eurolink Centre
49 Effra Road
London SW2 1BZ

Suites 139/140
Elm Park Mansions
Park Walk
LONDON
SW10 0AS

13th November 1997

Tel: 0171-352-9689
Fax: 0171-376-8378

Dear Polly,

Hey - really sorry I was in LA when you phoned this afternoon.

About the Di compassion video - it looks like a racing cert except for one small problem. We can't seem to get the Dean of St Paul's and Michael Winner on-side at the same time.

Not really the Dean's fault. The trouble is Michael's agent - a great sounding chick called Zoe who has a rather unusual way of managing her artistes.

Whatever the terms offered, she just stone-walls, sending back a card saying "God bless!" in red ink.

Well, I mean, that's nice, yeah, that's friendly, but it doesn't progress the negotiations any, am I right, Polly?

I'm about to write to her again, and I'll urge her on this occasion to reply with something more positive than "God bless!" on a card.

I hope to be sorted by Monday or Tuesday. Then I'll be in touch.

Have a great one!

Yours,

Liz

Liz Reed.

Directors: Jeff Boyd Liz Reed Martin Jacques
Simon King, Angela Picano (Sicily)
Registered in England NO: 2905691

Liz Reed
Heart Felt Productions Ltd.
Suites 139/140
Elm Park Mansions
London
SW10 0AS
13/11/97

November 18, 1997

Dear Liz,

Many thanks for your letter, keeping me up to date with the progress of your production. It sounds like you have a complicated production on your hands.

We are very pleased that Heart Film are happy for us to film and hope that Michael Winner is okay with this as well.

I look forward to hearing from you soon about the date.

With all best wishes

Polly Nash

**BRIGHTER
PICTURES LTD**
Television
and Film
Production
Eurolink Centre
49 Effra Road
London SW2 IBZ
Tel: 0171 738 4048
Fax: 0171 738 6212

Email: info@brighter-pictures.co.uk
Associate Office: 8205 Santica Monica Boulevard Suite 1427 Los Angeles California 90046-5967 Te: 213 960 5034
Reg. In England & Wales No:2597 443. Registered OfficeFiveChanceryLang Cliffords Inn London EC4A 1GU NO. 60789885

Heart Felt Productions Limited

'A Tragedy Aired is a Tragedy Shared'

Zoe
Michael Winner's Manager
The News Of The World
1 Virginia Street
London E1 9BD

Suites 139/140
Elm Park Mansions
Park Walk
LONDON
SW10 0AS

14th November 1997

Tel: 0171-352-9689
Fax: 0171-376-8378

Dear Zoe

'<u>DIANA COMPASSION VIDEO</u>.'

Great to get your card signally Michael's interest in our offer of 10th November.

That said, does "God Bless!" - while nice (don't get me wrong) - constitute a definite "yes"?

In any case, the scenario has slightly changed. As the enclosed letter from Brighter Pictures shows, Channel 4 are not involved, and this has caused us to alter our shooting schedule.

Channel 4 are now calling the shots and what they'd really like is to film Michael <u>with</u> Christina Hance, the artiste who is playing the role of Princess Di.

So, which dates would be favourite for Michael between now and 3rd December? Get back to me soonest if you could.

Hey - God bless you, too, Zoe!

Let's make a movie!

Yours,

Liz

Liz Reed.

Directors: Jeff Boyd Liz Reed Martin Jacques
Simon King, Angela Picano (Sicily)
Registered in England NO: 2905691

Thank you so much for writing. I really do appreciate it. It was very interesting to read what you had to say.

Good luck and God bless.

Zöe

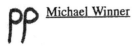 Michael Winner

1 Virginia Street, London E1 9BD

THE DEANERY
9 Amen Court
London
EC4M 7BU

From: The Dean of St Paul's
            The Very Revd Dr John Moses

Tel: 0171-236 2827
Fax: 0171-332 0298

14 November 1997

Liz Reed
Heart Felt Productions Limited
Suites 139/140
Elm Park Mansions
Park Walk
SW10 0AS

Dear Liz

Thank you for your letter of 11th November 1997. I am faxing this reply as it is so difficult to contact you by phone and earlier letters have been returned to us by the GPO marked *addressee unknown*.

The Dean is not now willing to take part in the video that has been the subject of earlier correspondence. We do feel that you are running serious risks here as there is every likelihood that the press will pick up on Christina Hance's involvement in the video and exploit the story to the full. We are sorry that this situation has arisen but I am sure you will appreciate that it does necessitate the Dean's withdrawal from the project.

Yours sincerely,

Anita Butt
Secretary to the Dean

Heart Felt Productions Limited

'A Tragedy Aired is a Tragedy Shared'

Mr Baz
Bazal
46/47 Bedford Square
London WC1 3DP

Suites 139/140
Elm Park Mansions
Park Walk
LONDON
SW10 0AS

15th November 1997

Tel: 0171-352-9689
Fax: 0171-376-8378

Dear Baz,

Really crap news about Liz, I'm afraid. The pressure has finally caught up with her. She's got what the medics call hormonal imbalance. This had led to testosterone overload. She insults everyone. Plus she twitches.

It's a form of Tourettes Syndrome, but more serious because she uses foul language in letters as well as face to face.

We've tried to put her in a clinic, but it seems that only she can make that decision (letter from medic enclosed).

I'm afraid she'll respond to yours of 14th November with a volley of abuse. Just ignore it. Or return to me marked 'Private and Confidential'.

Thanks for your help.
Yours,

Jeff Boyd.

Directors: Jeff Boyd Liz Reed Martin Jacques
Simon King, Angela Picano (Sicily)
Registered in England NO: 2905691

BAZAL

Nov. 18th '97

Jeff Boyd
Heartfelt Productions

Dear Jeff,

I was immensely touched by your letter about Mr. Reed's hormonal imbalance. This seems to be afflicting a number of T.V. women at the moment (cf Judy Finnigan). I enclose a couple of aspirin hoping they're of use. I certainly find they release the tension when I have "a bad month".

Yrs, BAZ

46/47 Bedford Square, London WC1B 3DP Telephone: +44 171 462 9462 Facsimile: +44 171 462 9998

Broadcast Communications plc trading as Bazal Productions Ltd
REGISTERED IN ENGLAND 1692513
REGISTERED OFFICE: 46/47 BEDFORD SQUARE, LONDON WC1B 3DP
VAT REGISTERED: 456 5371 34

Heart Felt Productions Limited

'A Tragedy Aired is a Tragedy Shared'

Mr Baz
Bazal Productions Ltd
46/47 Bedford Square
London WC1B 3DP

25th November 1997

Suites 139/140
Elm Park Mansions
Park Walk
LONDON
SW10 0AS
Tel: 0171-352-9689
Fax: 0171-376-8378

Dear Baz,

You and Jeff are literally shits, yeah. You've
been writing to each other, haven't you? About me.
Behind my <u>back</u>. I <u>know</u> you have.

So how do you think that makes me feel?

I'll tell you. It makes me feel like crap. That's
how it makes me feel. It makes me think my whole
life is down the fucking toilet.

God - you do your best, you start a company, you
have concepts, you pitch and access, propose and
progress, you don't take a holiday, you discover
your same sex partner is having it off with your
best friend, and as if that wasn't enough you find
out that colleagues and competitors are writing
letters to each other behind your back.

So thanks a <u>heap</u>, Baz.
I think I've had enough, I really do.
See ya around. Or probably not.

Liz

Liz Reed

PS. You don't happen to know anyone who might put
in a good word for Jeremy Isaacs, do you? We pilot
a rep rehab prog shortly for Radio 4 and we can't
find <u>anyone</u> who'll defend the man!

Heart Felt Productions Limited

'A Tragedy Aired is a Tragedy Shared'

David Hudson
Legal Affairs
The BBC
172-178 Victoria Road
London W3 6UL

Suites 139/140
Elm Park Mansions
Park Walk
LONDON
SW10 0AS

24th November 1997

Tel: 0171-352-9689
Fax: 0171-376-8378

Dear Mr Hudson

'ESTHER'

Thank you for your letter of 14th November, which seems to give us the green light to market a show under the above title.

'Two different shows with identical names,' you say, 'would detract from the BBC's goodwill.'

Precisely our intention!

Please be advised that we will be developing a show called 'ESTHER', fronted by Sarah, Duchess of York, for Dawn Airey at Channel 5.

If you have any other points to make, perhaps you could address them to Dawn. I shall be busy with the artistic side of the show - such as it is.

Yours sincerely,

Jeff Boyd.

Heart Felt Productions Limited

'A Tragedy Aired is a Tragedy Shared'

Will Wyatt
BBC Television
Wood Lane
London W12 7RJ

Suites 139/140
Elm Park Mansions
Park Walk
LONDON
SW10 0AS

24th November 1997

Tel: 0171-352-9689
Fax: 0171-376-8378

Dear Will,

Hi there! Listen – was mega impressed by something you said in today's Independent.

'Whether Bach is your bag or <u>Never Mind The Buzzcocks</u>, it is the range and quality of the BBC's output that has meant continued widespread support for our kind of broadcasting.'

Yeah yeah yeah!

Now. Could we quote this at the top of our letter-heads instead of the present message, 'A Tragedy Aired Is A Tragedy Shared' (a bit July/August 1996, right?)

Thus: 'Whether Bach is your bag or <u>Never Mind The Buzzcocks</u>, Heart Felt Deliver The Product You Want!'

We would attribute to you if you so specify.

Hey – have a great one, Will.

Yours,

Liz

Liz Reed.

Directors: Jeff Boyd Liz Reed Martin Jacques
Simon King, Angela Picano (Sicily)
Registered in England NO: 2905691

 **B B C** Broadcast

From the Chief Executive

2nd December 1997

Liz Reed
Heart Felt Productions Limited
Suites 139/140
Elm Park Mansions
Park Walk
LONDON
SW10 0AS

Dear Liz

Please accept this letter of confirmation that Will Wyatt is happy for you to use his quotation "Whether Bach is your Bag or Never Mind the Buzzcocks . . .".

Yours sincerely

Victoria Bowen
Secretary to Chief Executive, BBC Broadcast

Heart Felt Productions Limited
'WHETHER BACH IS YOUR BAG
OR <u>NEVER</u> <u>MIND</u> <u>THE</u> <u>BUZZCOCKS'</u>
HEART FELT DELIVERS

Victoria Bowen   139/140 Elm Park Mansions
BBC Broadcast   Park walk
Broadcasting House   London SW10 0AS
London W1A 1AA
3rd December   Tel: 0171 352 9689
                              Fax; 376 8378

Dear Victoria,

Hey - many thanks. And thank Will too, yeah? It
looks really great.

There is something you can do for me. Do you or
Will happen to know anyone who might put in a good
word for Jeremy Isaacs in a repu rehab docu we're
doing for Radio 4? We're getting desperate!

Hope to hear from you, and ta ever so again

Be nice

Yours,

Liz

Liz Reed

Directors: Jeff Boyd Liz Reed Martin Jacques
Simon King, Angela Picano (Sicily)
Registered in England NO: 2905691

LOOK ALIKES

THE ORIGINAL AND STILL THE BEST

13 Cinnamon Row Plantation Wharf London SW11 3TW
Telephone: 0171-924 4447 Fax No: 1071-924 2662

With Compliments

Hi Liz

Please add to your files!

Regards
Kara

QUEEN MOTHER

Gladys Crosbie

Heart Felt Productions Limited

'A Tragedy Aired is a Tragedy Shared'

Karen Black
LOOK-ALIKES
13 Cinnamon Row
Plantation Wharf
London SW11 3TW

Suites 139/140
Elm Park Mansions
Park Walk
LONDON
SW10 0AS

7th December 1997

Tel: 0171-352-9689
Fax: 0171-376-8378

Dear Karen

'<u>GOD BLESS YOU, MA'AM!</u>'

Hi there! Many thanks for sending me Gladys Crosbie's photo and CV. She looks spot-on to play the Queen Mother in our memorial CD and video.

But hey – just one small point, Karen. Gladys isn't a tart, is she? Or a drug-fiend?

OK, so she looks perfectly respectable, but that's what we thought about Christina, yeah?

Sorry to be faddy about this, Karen, but I don't want another of my developments to go belly up because one of your artistes has been putting it about.

Let's make money! Top! Mad for it!

Ever,

Liz

Liz Reed.

Directors: Jeff Boyd Liz Reed Martin Jacques
Simon King, Angela Picano (Sicily)
Registered in England NO: 2905691

Heart Felt Productions Limited

'A Tragedy Aired is a Tragedy Shared'

Jane Butterworth

Suites 139/140
Elm Park Mansions
Park Walk
LONDON
SW10 0AS

9th December 1997

Tel: 0171-352-9689
Fax: 0171-376-8378

Dear Jane,

Oh dear. Rather bad news about Liz, I'm afraid. The pressure has been getting to her more and more lately, and yesterday we were finally compelled to pop her into the Charter Clinic in Lisson Grove.

Not really your fault, Jane, though perhaps you could have shown her a little more understanding over your scripts for 'WHO PUT HEROIN IN MY KIDDIES' SWEETS?' In fact, I have some sympathy with your position and have managed to persuade David Liddiment that a further re-write should be done before recording, and that your views should be borne in mind.

I will be in touch with you again once this re-write has been carried out.

Meanwhile, should you wish to get in touch with Liz, her address is:

> Charter Nightingale Clinic
> 11-19 Lisson Grove
> London NW1 6SH

She will be under sedation for a few days, but when she is feeling a little stronger I'm sure she'd love to hear from you.

The show must go on!

Yours,

Jeff Boyd.

Directors: Jeff Boyd Liz Reed Martin Jacques
Simon King, Angela Picano (Sicily)
Registered in England NO: 2905691

British Broadcasting Corporation Broadcasting House Portland Place London W1A 1AA Telephone 0171 580 4468 Fax 0171 765 3822

B B C RADIO 4

Ms Liz Reed

Heartfelt Productions Limited
Suites 139/140
Elm Park Mansions, Park Walk
London SW10 0AS

22nd December 1997

Dear Liz

January 1998 Commissioning Round

In consultation with Caroline Elliot, I have now completed my review of Radio 4's requirements for the forthcoming commissioning round and, with regret, our decision is that you will not be invited to submit proposals in this commissioning round. However, I would stress that this decision relates to this round and does not in any way preclude you from submitting proposals through other suppliers or from being considered for inclusion in future.

The review was based on information on file and I note that you failed to complete and return a copy of the questionnaire sent out by Caroline Elliot in November. I now enclose a further copy for completion and return to Caroline Elliot by 19th January 1998.

As I have previously explained, Caroline Elliot and I will continue to review the list of those invited to submit proposals as we enter each commissioning phase. As you would expect, the list will change to some degree with each commissioning phase, thus reflecting the slots available. Radio 4 will adopt a rolling commissioning system next year and we are currently consulting on how this ought to operate. The next review will take place at the point that we instigate this new system.

I will be writing to all suppliers who have expressed a continuing interest in Radio 4 to update the position before the next commissioning phase.

In the meantime, if there is anything which you wish to record for consideration in our next review, please write to Caroline Elliot, Network Manager, at the above address.

Thank you for your continuing interest in Radio 4.

James Boyle
Controller, Radio 4

Heart Felt Productions Limited
'STILL ON FILE WITH RADIO 4! YEAH!'

James Boyle
BBC Radio 4
Broadcasting House
London W1A 1AA

Suites 139/140
Elm Park Mansions
Park Walk
LONDON
SW10 0AS

5th January 1998

Tel: 0171-352-9689
Fax: 0171-376-8378

Dear James,

Thanks for yours of 22nd December addressed to Liz.

Liz isn't with us anymore. She got barking disease. She barked at people in the street and swore at them on the telephone. She would pull a major player out of a meeting and call him a tub of shit on his mobile phone.

This had a negative effect on our profile. It was bad too for the BBC. We're on file with Radio 4. Every time Liz called a major player a tub of shit on his mobile phone it reflected badly on the BBC.

We had to get rid of her.

Going through her stuff, I discovered that one of her projects was for you and Caroline Eliot. 'WITH FRIENDS LIKE THIS . . . .'

Kind of ironic, yeah? Anyway, she was getting nowhere with it. No one would speak up for Jeremy Isaacs. She wrote to Lord Deedes, Lord Windlesham, Sir Anthony Dowell, Bamber Gascoigne . . . . .

Hey - it would be quicker to tell you who she <u>didn't</u> write to!

Not one person volunteered to defend Jeremy! (I enclose a copy of a letter from Sir Anthony Dowell. Too busy! That's what they all said!)

So that one went pear-shaped. Never mind. Nil desperandum. Thanks for the Questionnaire. I'll fill this in and return it to Caroline before 19th February.

Let's keep in touch, James.

Yours,

Jeff Boyd.
Enc. Letter from Sir Anthony Dowell.

Directors: Jeff Boyd Liz Reed Martin Jacques
Simon King, Angela Picano (Sicily)
Registered in England NO: 2905691

Sir Anthony Dowell, CBE
Director

Liz Reed,
Heart Felt Productions Ltd.,   22nd September 1997
Suites 139/140
Elm Park Mansions,
Park Walk,
London, SW10 0AS.

Dear Liz Reed,

Thank you for your letter to Sir Anthony. Unfortunately, our Christmas schedule is extremely hectic and Sir Anthony is rehearsing and performing throughout. He is, therefore, unable to give any interviews during this period.

Yours sincerely,

Jeanetta Laurence,
Artistic Administrator.

Royal Opera House Covent Garden London WC2E 9DD Telephone (44) 171 240 1200 Facsimile (44) 171 212 9121
Barons Court Rehersal Studios: Telephone (44) 181 748 8765 Facsimile (44) 741 4234
Press Office: Direct Line (44) 171 212 9165 Facsimile(44) 171 379 7059

Registered inEngland No: 480523 Registered Office as SHOWN Charity Registered No: 211775

17th November 1997

Room 3218
BBC White City
201 Wood Lane
London
W12 7RJ

Tel: 0181 752 5766
Fax: 0181 752 4090

Liz Reed
Heart Felt Productions Ltd
Suites 139/140
Elm Park Mansions
Park Walk
London
SW10 0AS

Dear Liz

Thank you for sending in your proposal **Must Have/Must Do**. Nicola Moody, Deputy Head of Independent Commissioning Group, Factual and the other Commissioning Executives have discussed your idea and, as the Development Team, we are now replying on their behalf.

Unfortunately ICG Factual is not currently looking for a new prime time magazine show for the BBC. As a general guide however, the BBC has tried to target youth audiences in the past but audience research has shown that that younger audiences tend to watch the same television programmes as everyone else. With this in mind, we wouldn't be interested in any programme targeted so specifically at such a narrow age group.

Good luck elsewhere.

Kind regards,

Alex Greenwood
Proposals Co-ordinator

Michael Tait
Development Co-ordinator

Charter Nightingale Hospital

11-19 Lisson Grove
London NW1 6SH
Telephone: 0171-258 3828
Facsimile: 0171-724 8294

Alex Greenwood
The BBC
Wood Lane
London W12 7RJ

28th January 1998

Dear Alex,

Hi there! It's me again! Got your letter of 17th November 1997 about 'MUST HAVE, MUST DO'. Thanks. I'd have answered sooner, but guess what.

For the past ten weeks I've been a patient here at the Charter Clinic Lisson Grove!

Yeah really. We must share some time. My sponsor says I must share with as many people as possible. Anyway, the good news is that, while I'll never be cured, I am in recovery and able once again to pitch and develop.

You say in your letter that the BBC has discovered that there's no point in targeting a youth audience. Interesting. Does David Liddiment know this, do you think? He and the Network are going flat out for an 18-30 demographic. Are things about to go belly up for David?

Anyway, this one will hit the spot, Alex. '<u>GIN AND BEAR IT, MA'AM!</u>' That's right, a musical tribute to the Queen Mum, featuring all her fave artistes. Vera Lynn, Ray Allen and Lord Charles, the Roly Polys and Dawn French.

As you probably know, we had been progressing 'GOD BLESS YOU, MA'AM!', a memorial CD and video to be released on her death, but because of her recent hip operation we thought it best to cash in now.

How about 'HIP HIP HOORAY!' as an alternative title?

'Get well soon, Queen Mum
You're really supersonic!
Make a quick recovery
And you can have your gin and tonic!'

Let's hit the ground running, Alex!

Yours in recovery,

Liz Reed.

British **Broadcasting Corporation** Broadcasting House Portland Place London W1A 1AA
Telephone 0171 580 4468 Fax 0171 765 3822

Independents' Commissioning Group, Factual

Liz Reed   26 February 1998
Heart Felt Productions Ltd
138/140 Elm Park Mansions
Park Walk
London SW10 0AS

Dear Liz

Re: 'Gin and Bear It, Ma'am!'

Thank you for sending in your proposal about a musical tribute to the Queen Mum. It has
been discussed with Nicola Moody, Deputy Head of Independent Commissioning Group,
Factual and the other Commissioning Executives and, as Proposals Co-ordinator, I am replying on their behalf.

Unfortunately we have just had a project about the Queen Mother commissioned. While our
project is rather more of a historical profile than a tribute to Her Highness, we do feel that it
would be very difficult for us to push another Queen Mother project through the system.
You could try writing to Trevor Dann, Head of Musical Entertainment at the BBC, who
might be able to help you find a slot for 'Gin and Bear It, Ma'am!'

I hope you are feeling better now and we all look forward to receiving your next idea.

Kind regards,

Alex

Alex Greenwood
Proposals Co-ordinator

Sarah, Duchess of York
Sunninghill Park
Sunninghill
Berkshire

Charter Nightingale Hospital

11-19 Lisson Grove
London NW1 6SH
Telephone: 0171-258 3828
Facsimile: 0171-724 8294

30th January 1998

Dear Sarah,

Hey – your appearance on the Larry King Chat Show really really moved me.

"I'm getting stronger, Larry," you said. "I'm healing."

Thank you for sharing this with us, Sarah. You spoke for women everywhere. I <u>know</u>. I've been there. I've got the scars. I've got the T-shirt. But – hey – I'm healing too. For the past ten weeks I've been a patient here at the Charter Nightingale Clinic, Lisson Grove. But I don't want to burden you with that. It wouldn't be fair.

It's just that the Charter Nightingale was one of Diana's most fave charities and I know she'd want you to be supportive of one of its patients. That's what she would have done. She'd have been there for me. But I don't want to talk about that. Really.

It's just that one of the last things Diana said to me was: "Hey, Liz, if anything happens to me and you need help, get in touch with Sarah. She won't let you down. Sarah and I are partners."

But I don't want to mention that. Really. I want to talk about my latest TV development for Dawn Airey at Channel 5. Entitled 'ESTHER' (we've been able to franchise the title from the BBC), it's to be the ultimate caring show, a prime-time opportunity for women to share their grief with the nation.

At the moment, Dawn and I are mulling over possible presenters and it's between you and Tragic TV Paula. Dawn favours Tragic TV Paula but I favour you because you're fatter. That's important. OK, you're not as fat as TV Vanessa, but who is? Roy Hudd isn't as fat as TV Vanessa. But you're fatter than Tragic TV Paula.

So – how about it, Sarah? It would be a great vehicle for you if you want to do confessional TV in this country. Plus there'd be mega-bucks in it.

Hey – one day at a time, yeah.

Yours,

Liz

Liz Reed.

Charter Medical of England Ltd., No. 1431836. Registered in England, 1-5 Radnor Walk, London SW3 4BP

9th February 1998

Dear Miss Med,

The Duchess of York has asked me to write and thank you for your recent letter, and I apologise that your first letter remained unanswered.

The Duchess was touched that you took the time and trouble to write and tell her about your idea for a new TV show. However The Duchess is not in a position to undertake any new projects at the moment and I am sorry to have to send you such a disappointing reply.

This letter comes with The Duchess's very best wishes, and thank you for thinking of her.

Yours sincerely,

Hilary Bett

Miss Hilary Bett,
Personal Assistant to The Duchess of York

Heart Felt Productions Limited

'A Tragedy Aired is a Tragedy Shared'

Dawn Airey
Channel 5 Television
22 Long Acre
London WC2

18th February 1998

Suites 139/140
Elm Park Mansions
Park Walk
LONDON
SW10 0AS
Tel: 0171-352-9689
Fax: 0171-376-8378

Dear Dawn

Hi there! As you can see I'm out of the clinic at last and back at work! Hey – how fab is that?

Nothing of any great import to conceptualise at this moment in time so I'm just touching base.

Watching TV again after three months in recovery, it occurs to me that there is just one area in which Channel 5 might smarten up its act.

I think the links could be a little sassier, a little more now, a little more in ya face. Here are two suggestions:

1. Introducing the rugger at 6pm on Sundays, the guy or gal doing the link should say:

"And now – over to the men with the funny shaped balls!"

2. Introducing Melinda Messenger on the Jack Docherty Show, the guy or gal doing the link should say:

"I'm sure there'll be a couple of <u>interesting points</u> during that conversation!"

OK, OK – own up time. I got those one-liners from Denise Van Outen (and is <u>she</u> one smart telly babe!) but you can have them for free!

Hey – just one thing more. You'll be pondering why my former partner, Jeff Boyd, has been struck off the letterhead. He's no longer with us, Dawn. He got a pull crossing the Channel with a kilo of coke in his trousers. I wonder who tipped off Customs – not!

So <u>he</u> won't be giving it large down the Met Bar after TFI Friday. HA!
One day at a time, yeah.
Yours,

Liz Reed.

Directors: Liz Reed Martin Jacques
Simon King, Angela Picano (Sicily)
Registered in England NO: 2905691

Heart Felt Productions Limited

'A Tragedy Aired is a Tragedy Shared'

Colin Jarvis
BBC Worldwide
80 Wood Lane
London W2

18th February 1998

Suites 139/140
Elm Park Mansions
Park Walk
LONDON
SW10 0AS
Tel: 0171-352-9689
Fax: 0171-376-8378

Dear Colin

Hi there! Hey - really agreed with what you said in yesterday's Independent about the damage done to Brit coms by the Americans.

OK, so we know they have no sense of irony on the other side of the herring pond.

Like what else is new?

But are there any other reasons why Yank writers simply don't 'get' classic Brit fare such as 'Men Behaving Badly'. whereas the writers of, say, 'Dressing For Breakfast', 'Holding the Baby' or 'Faith In The Future' would improve 'Seinfeld', 'Frasier' or 'The Larry Sanders Show' out of all recognition.

Do you know who I mean by Marks and Gran? Take the following classic exchanges:

Classic Exchange 1: Wimpish ex-husband hurts hand on fridge door when calling on ex-wife.

Husband: Ouch!

Wife: Can you wiggle your fingers?

Husband: I'm not in the mood for foreplay!!!

Classic Remark 2. Ext. Country house cricket field. Oswald Mosley batting. Foppish invert arrives by car.

Invert: Oswald! Have you got middle and leg?

Why can't the writers of 'Seinfeld' come up with stuff like that? We've been commissioned to examine the problem in a documentary for Channel 4 entitled 'JUST WHAT <u>IS</u> IT WITH THE AMERICANS?' As the guy who sells Brit formats to the yanks would you appear on the programme. Filming in May.
Have a great one!
Yours,

Liz

Liz Reed.

Directors: Liz Reed Martin Jacques
Simon King, Angela Picano (Sicily)
Registered in England NO: 2905691

British Broadcasting Corporation BBC Worldwide Limited Woodlands 80 Wood Lane London W12 0TT
Telephone: +44 181 576 2490 Fax: +44 181 740 1182

B B C Worldwide

FACSIMILE TRANSMISSION

TO: Liz Reed – Heart Felt Productions Ltd

FROM: Alec La Ronde   FAX: 0171 376 8378

DATE: 24.02.1998   e-mail: alec.la-ronde@bbc.co.uk

RE: What is it With The Americans?

PAGES: 1

This facsimile is intended for the above recipient only and may be privileged or confidential. If this transmission has been sent to you in error please contact us immediately and ensure that its contents are not disclosed.

Dear Liz,

Thank you for your fax to Mary Collins on 21.02.1998.

Colin will be happy to participate.

Best regards,

Alec La Ronde
Format Licensing

BBC Worldwide Limited is a subsidiary of the British Broadcasting Corporation
Registered Number: 1420028 England Registered Office Woodlands 80 Wood Lane London W12 0TT

Heart Felt Productions Limited

'WHETHER BACH IS YOUR BAG
OR <u>NEVER</u> <u>MIND</u> <u>THE</u> <u>BUZZCOCKS!</u>'
HEART FELT WILL DELIVER
(Will Wyatt.The BBC. The Best!)

Geoffrey Perkins
Mr Comedy!   Elm Park Mansions
BBC Television   Park Walk
London W12   London SW10 0AS

19th February   Tel: 0171-352-9689

Dear Geoffrey
<u>'CRAPPYFRUIT AND PINK KNICKERS!'</u>

Hi there! Sorry I haven't been pitching lately, but I've been in recovery! I've been in the Charter Clinic,Lisson Grove.

Part history. This one will blow your skirt up, Geoffrey. A celeb food quiz featuring a bald presenter with a speech impediment, two team captains and low rent guests with a wacky sense of humour(eg Bill Oddie).

'Which Dish Is Real?' That wil be one of the games. One contestant will describe a breakfast cereal he was given in Sweden called 'CRAPPYFRUIT'! Another says she was given a milkshake in Norway called 'PINK KNICKERS'! Which is true and which is false? Hilarious right? And kinda sexy too if, say,one of the team captains was Sara Cox. Hey - imagine the fun we could get out of Coxy talking about her pink knickers.

Here's another angle. In the studio a French chef (beret, onions round his neck) is happy to be ribbed by our bald presenter. A blindfolded guest will be fed something dis- gusting by our garlicky 'ami' from Paris. This will give rise to the following hilarious exchange:

Guest: "Crickey! What's that?"
Comic French chef: "Les frogs legs, oui?"
Guest: "Oh <u>Yuk!</u>"
Bald presenter:"And this from the country whose idea of toilet sophistication is a hole in the ground!"
What do you say, Geoffrey? We're ready to pilot!
Yours,

Liz

Liz Reed

Directors: Jeff Boyd Liz Reed Martin Jacques
Simon King, Angela Picano (Sicily)
Registered in England NO: 2905691

Heart Felt Productions Limited

'A Tragedy Aired is a Tragedy Shared'

Francesca Liversidge
Transworld
61-63 Uxbridge Road
London W5 5SA

19th February 1998

Suites 139/140
Elm Park Mansions
Park Walk
LONDON
SW10 0AS
Tel: 0171-352-9689
Fax: 0171-376-8378

Dear Francesca
'SMILE PLEASE!'

Hi there! Here's the story. We're basically filming a six-parter on the nature of celebrity for Dawn Airey at Channel 5. In prog 1, Mark Lawson says you paid £250,000 for hairdresser Nicky Clarke's first book.

"We'd all like some of that," quips Mark. "I fancy being paid £250,000 for cutting someone's hair."

Not sure what Mark's point is, and that's not why I'm writing. Here's what I want to know. Throughout the programme, your author is described as a 'celebrity hairdresser'. Does this mean that he's a hairdresser to celebrities or a celebrity himself? I think it's the former but I was at the Met Bar with Coxy on Friday night and she thinks it's the latter. (She's a one off, Coxy. They broke the mould when they made Coxy).

I mean it's totally ambiguous yeah. A celebrity chef can usually cook a bit, but a chicken farmer is seldom if ever a chicken. On the chicken analogy Nicky isn't himself a celeb. So who's right? Me or Coxy? We don't want to commit a solipsism in the very first programme.

The series will emphasise the point that in 1998 it's more about how we look than who we really are. I gather that you got Nicky's book because his agent, Luigi Bonomi, held a beauty contest among publishers and you won!

Great! Is that how you get all your books? Would you come on the show and talk about it? (Hey - small wonder Random House aren't getting any big books! Howzabout Gail's new hair-style? No no no!)

One last thing. We're tri-media here, Francesca, currently pro-gressing two toilet books for the Christmas Humour Shelves - 'HOW TO TELL IF YOUR PARENTS AREN'T ON DRUGS' and 'THE LITTLE BOOK OF REALLY GREAT NEWS JUST WHEN YOU THOUGHT YOUR LIFE WAS DOWN THE TOILET'. Would you like to read them?
Have a great one, Francesca!
Yours,

Liz
Liz Reed.

Directors: Liz Reed Martin Jacques
Simon King, Angela Picano (Sicily)
Registered in England NO: 2905691

T R A N S W O R L D   P U B L I S H I N G   L T D

F A X   T R A N S M I S S I O N

TO   Winston Obogo
CC
FROM   Dan Hammond
NO OF PAGES (including this one) 1
DATE   May 15, 1998
SUBJECT HOW TO TELL YOUR PARENTS ARE ON DRUGS: THE
LITTLE BOOK OF GREAT NEWS

Thank you for sending the above title to Francesca Liversidge for consideration. She will get back to you as soon as she has had a chance to read it.

With best wishes

Dan Hammond
BANTAM EDITORIAL DEPARTMENT

CORGI BANTAM BLACK SWAN ANCHOR BANTAM PRESS PARTRIDGE PRESS DOUBLEDAY EXPERT
CHILDRENS BOOKS (BANTAM CORGI & DOUBLEDAY)

61-63 UXBRIDGE ROAD LONDON W5 53A ENGLAND TEL: + 44 (01) 81 579 2652 FAX: 44 (01) 81 575 5479
E-MAIL : INFO@TRANSWORLD.PUBLISHERS.CO.UK

Heart Felt Productions Limited

'WHETHER BACH IS YOUR BAG
OR NEVER MIND THE BUZZCOCKS!'
HEART FELT WILL DELIVER

Jools Barringer
Ginger Productions
131 Great Portland Street
London W1P 8DB
20th February 1998
Dear Jools,

139/140 Elm Park Mansions
Park Walk
London SW10 0AS
Tel: 0171 352 9689
Fax: 0171 376 8378

Hey, really sorry I haven't been in touch lately. You were mega-helpful last year when I wrote to you about our compassion video tribute to Diana, Princess of Wales.

We wanted this to have a light touch, so we asked Chris to advise on surreal humour. You know the kinda thing - like when he goes down the Met Bar with Gazza and Danny Baker and they're wearing women's boobs outside their England strips!

OK, basically we've been commissioned by Dawn Airey at Channel 5 to do a five-part documentary on The British Sense of Humour.

One idea we'll be examining is that celebs must demonstrate a sense of humour by opening their mouths very widely when another celeb cracks a gag.

Those who have mastered the celeb laugh include the Duchess of York, Ainsley Harriott and Richard Branson.

I enclose a really great photo of Richard in bed with your boss, the Mad-Cap Ginger Nut! Obviously TV Chris has cracked a top gag to make Richard break up like this. But what?

One of the features in the show will be a competition called 'Guess The Punchline!', in which viewers will be invited to supply the tag to celebrity wisecracks.

We'd like to use this photo in the show, if we can find out what TV Chris's wisecrack was. It must have been a great gag to cause Richard to open his mouth as wide as this. 'Corpsing's' really great because it shows celebs can 'relax' just like ordinary people.

Can TV Chris remember what the wisecrack was? Could you ask him, Jools. I'd be grateful!
Hey - have a good one!
Yours,

Liz

Liz Reed.

Directors: Jeff Boyd Liz Reed Martin Jacques
Simon King, Angela Picano (Sicily)
Registered in England NO: 2905691

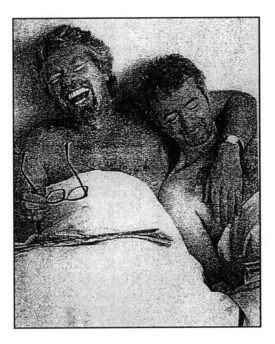

ginger

Television *Productions LTD*

Liz Reed
Heart Felt Productions Limited
Suites 139/140
Elm Park Mansions
Park Wak
London
SW10 0AS

24 January 1998

Dear Liz

Thank you very much for writing in to Chris, describing the format for your new five-part Channel 5 documentary. Congratuations on the commission! Unfortunately Chris is unable to help you with your enquiry; he does not remember the conversation he was having with Richard Branson when the photo was taken.

However, we wish you lots of luck with your production and every success in the future.

Your sincerely

Jools Barringer
Assistant to Chris Evans

The Media Centre, 3rd Floor, 131-151 Great Titchfield Street, London W1P 8PB

tel: 0171-577 7100 fax: 0171-577 7101

Ginger Television Productions Ltd director chris evans, registered in england company no 2818556

registered office paramount house, 102-170 Wardour street, london W1V 3a6

Heart Felt Productions Limited

'A Tragedy Aired is a Tragedy Shared'

Eddie Bell
Harper Collins
77-85 Fulham Palace Road
London W6 8JB

Suites 139/140
Elm Park Mansions
Park Walk
LONDON
SW10 0AS
Tel: 0171-352-9689
Fax: 0171-376-8378

4th March 1998

Dear Eddie

'SMILE PLEASE!'

OK, basically we've been commissioned by Dawn Airey of
Channel 5 to do a six-part series on the nature of celebrity.

In Episode 1 we will discuss the fact that for wannabees in
1998 it's not about who you really are but about how you
look.

One guest in this episode will be Luigi Bonomi, the liter-
ary agent, who sells books only to good-looking publishers.

Before selling the memoirs of Nicky Clarke, the celeb hairdresser, Luigi held a beauty contest, which was won easily
by Francesca Liversidge. She's with Bantam, Eddie. (Hey – no
wonder Random House aren't getting any big books. They may
be unpleasant but they aren't good-looking!)

Anyway, I wonder what you think of Luigi's practice, Eddie?
Is it your policy at Harper Collins these days to publish
only the young and beautiful?

Hey – perhaps that's why you dropped Chris Patten! You said
his book was boring and badly written, but I bet that was
just an excuse. He writes as well as Tragic TV Paula, and
you published her. I bet you published Tragic TV Paula
because she's better looking than Chris Patten!

Anyway – would you come on the show and talk about it,
Eddie? We could film you in your office if that suited you
best.

Oh – and one other favour. Could you forward the enclosed
letter to Tragic TV Paula? I haven't got her address. Ta!
Have a great one!
Yours,

Liz Reed.

Directors: Jeff Boyd Liz Reed Martin Jacques
Simon King, Angela Picano (Sicily)
Registered in England NO: 2905691

Heart Felt Productions Limited

' A tragedy Aired is a Tragedy Shared'

Paula Yates	Suites 139/140
c/o Harper Collins	Elm Park Mansions
77-85 Fulham Palace Road	Park Walk
London	LONDON
W6 8JB	SW10 0AS
4th March	Tel: 0171-352-9689
	Fax: 0171-376-8378

Dear Paula

Hey- really empathised with your recent celeb interview in OK magazine.

"I'll never speak to Geldof again" you said.
Thank you for sharing that with us Paula. I think that's what we were all wondering. A few of us were hanging out down Cloud 9 on Saturday (deep house and techno with Sally Manda, Shifta and Moveya - hey are they good or what?) Anyway we kept turning to each other and saying:

"Hey - will tragic TV Paula ever speak to Geldof again? That's what I would like to know."
When you feel strong enough to do TV again here's one you might want to consider. We've been commissioned by Dawn Airey at Channel 5 to produce a fly-on-the-wall grief counselling entertainment to be called either 'ESTHER' or 'VANESSA'.

We have been able to franchise the title 'ESTHER' from the BBC, but are now wondering whether it would be better to sub-let the title 'VANESSA' from Anglia TV. OK, so Esther's been at it for longer than Vanessa, but Vanessa is fatter. That's important. You can't be too fat for an early evening grief show.

At the moment, Dawn and I are mulling over possible presenters for 'ESTHER' (or 'VANESSA') and it's between you and Sarah, Duchess of York. Can I put your name forward, Paula?
I'm sending this via your publisher Harper Collins, so I hope it reaches you. I look forward to hearing from you.

Hey one day at a time, yeah
Yours,

Li
Liz Reed

Directors: Jeff Boyd Liz Reed Martin Jacques
Simon King, Angela Picano (Sicily)
Registered in England NO: 2905691

A Division o
Harper Collins *Pubishers*

7-85 Fulham Palace Road
Hammersmith
London W3 3JB

Telephone 0181-741 7070
Facsimile: 0181 307 4440

HarperCollins *Publishers*

13 March 1998

Liz Reed
Heart Felt Productions Limited
Suites 139/140
Elm Park Mansions
Park Walk
LONDON SW10 0AS

Dear Liz,

Thank you for your letter to Eddie Bell dated 4 March 1998.

Apologies for not replying sooner but as you probably are aware, events did overtake us for a while.

Eddie has asked me to reply to you to thank you but to decline your kind invitation to meet.

Yours sincerely,

Linda Lord-Hogan
PA to Chairman

Registered as Harper Collins *Publishers* Ltd Scotland 1949 No: 273891, Westerhill Road, Bishopbriggs, Glasgow

Heart Felt Productions Limited

'A Tragedy Aired is a Tragedy Shared'

Mrs Anita Butt
The Deanery
9 Amen Court
London EC4M 7BU

Suites 139/140
Elm Park Mansions
Park Walk
LONDON
SW10 0AS

7th April 1998

Tel: 0171-352-9689
Fax: 0171-376-8378

Dear Mrs Butt,

Hi there! It's me again! Guess what. For the past three
months I've been a patient at the Charter Clinic, Lisson
Grove. Yeah really. We must share some time. My sponsor
says I must share with as many people as possible.

Anyway. Past history. End of story. Finito. La la la. I'm
up and rarin' to go!

Here's the hot goss: since our tribute to Diana, Princess
of Wales went pear-shaped (not really the Dean's fault),
we have devoted our energies to GIN AND BEAR IT, MA'AM!'
- a musical tribute to the Queen Mum, featuring all her
most fave artistes. Vera Lynn, Ray Allen and Lord
Charles, The Black and White Minstrels, the Roly Polys,
Brian Blessed (recitations) and Dawn French.

We had planned it for TV but, alas, have been told by
them (letter enclosed) that the BBC has already commissioned a tribute. They suggest we pitch it to Trevor
Dann, Head of Music for BBC Radio, and this we have done.

And guess what! Trevor is mad keen that the Dean fronts
the show, as he would have the Di tribute had it not gone
down the toilet!

Isn't that great!

Flag me soonest if you think we have a show.

Very best wishes.

Yours,

Liz

Liz Reed.

Directors: Jeff Boyd Liz Reed Martin Jacques
Simon King, Angela Picano (Sicily)
Registered in England NO: 2905691

THE DEANERY
9 Amen Court
London
EC4M 7BU

Tel: 0171-236 2827
Fax: 0171-332 0298

From: The Dean of St Paul's
          The Very Revd Dr John Moses

21st April 1998

Liz Reed
Heart Felt Productions Ltd
Suites 139/140
Elm Park Mansions
Park Walk
SW10 0AS

Dear Liz

Thank you for your letter of 7th April. Sorry to hear that you have been out of action for a while. I hope you are now feeling much better.

I'm afraid this will be disappointing news but the Dean has asked me to say that he will not be able to contribute to the new video you are planning about the Queen Mother.

With best wishes,

Yours sincerely,

Anita Butt

Secretary to the Dean.

HEART FELT PRODUCTIONS

Suites 139-140
Elm Park Mansion
Park Walk
London SW10 0AS

Tel: 0171 352 9689
Fax: 0171 376 8378

Directors:
Steve Oboto
Ainsley Parrott
Winston Obogo
Simone Durity
P. Amin

Keith Hellawell QPM
Drug Tzar!
Government Offices
Great George Street
London SW1P 3AL
8th April 1998

Dear Chief Constable

'YOU'S BUSTED, MY MAN!'

So - you turned down our invite to appear on the above programme last October. Hey - no sweat. Your prerogative, my man.

Your recent attempt to bridge the generation gap by talking
about drugs to young people has prompted us to write again.

Why did you address young people, Chief Constable? What do
young people know about drugs?

Jack squat! They've only just started using them.

If you want to wise up on drugs you should talk to my ol'
grandaddy and to my ol' grandaddy's friends. My ol' grandaddy
and my ol' grandaddy's friends have been on the pipe for thir-
ty, forty years.

We can help. We have recently produced a pamphlet entitled
'HOW TO TELL IF YOUR PARENTS AREN'T ON DRUGS'. We will be
distributing this outside school playgrounds and are currently
negotiating with Dawn Airey at Channel 5 to turn it into a TV
documentary.

I enclose extracts which I hope will be of interest.
I also enclose a photographic cover image. You will agree, I
think, that no one on drugs would appear like this in public.
I look forward to your comments, Chief Constable.
One day at a time, my man!

Winston Obogo
Winston Obogo

Keith HelawellQPM
UK Anti-Drugs Co-ordinator
Room 60a/2
Government Offices
Great George Street
London SW1P 3AL

Tel: 0171 270 5399
Fax: 0171 270 5857

RC 438

Winston Obogo
Heartfelt Productions Limited
Suites 139/140
Elm Park Mansions
Park Walk
London SW10 0AS

30 April 1998

Dear Mr Obogo

Thank you for your letter dated 8 April to Mr Hellawell. He has noted your concerns and is grateful for the update on the work that you are doing. He has asked me to pass on his best wishes in your future endeavours.

Sincerely

Ronnie Clarke

RONNIE CLARKE
SPS/MR HELLAWELL

HEART FELT PRODUCTIONS

Suites 139-140
Elm Park Mansion
Park Walk
London SW10 0AS

Tel: 0171 352 9689
Fax: 0171 376 8378

Andrew Marr
The Independent
1 Canada Square
London E14

Directors:
Steve Oboto
Ainsley Parrott
Winston Obogo
Simone Durity
P. Amin

7th April 1998

Dear Andy

'YOU'S BUSTED, MY MAN!'

Word up! Our present development is the above for Dawn Airey
at Channel 5 (formerly entitled 'The Day My Whole World
Collapsed', featuring Tragic TV Patsy Palmer, troubled funnyman Michael Barrymore and Tragic Bra Beauty Sophie Anderton).

Guest speakers are to be Drug Tzar, Chief Constable Hellawell,
and the Rt Hon Michael Portillo.

Last week a journalist on your paper (Gerard Gilbert) said
that watching Channel 5 was the most fun to be had without
taking drugs.

This gives out the wrong signals to old people, Andy, many of
whom have been trying to give up drugs since 1966.

Plus there is the embarrassment of his having said it about
Channel 5. When the programme is broadcast, Channel 5's hand-
ful of viewers might take Gerard's advice, switch off the TV,
hire a taxi and get on one down at the Leopard Lounge.

Would you come on the programme and say that Gerard must have
been off his face to say such a thing?

Perhaps you could bone up on the following argument to be put
to Chief Constable Hellawell by one of the brothers. It's more
dangerous to be in police custody than to take Ecstasy.

Deaths from Ecstasy since 1990 - 58. Deaths in police custody
since 1990 - 147.
Peace, my man.

Winston Obogo.
cc. Dawn Airey. Channel 5.

THE INDEPENDENT

15 April 1998

Winston Obogo
Heart Felt Productions Limited
Suites 139/140
Elm Park Mansions
Park Walk
London SW10 0AS

Dear Winston Obogo

Many thanks for the letter.

I don't want to attack Gerard by name; I don't think it helps morale here if the boss publicly kicks reviewers. But of course I do disagree with him and I'm very happy to explain why I don't think that legalising drugs helps at all. If that's any good to you, give us a ring, by all means.

Yours ever

Andrew Marr
Editor-in-Chief

NEWSPAPER PUBLISHING PLC
One Canada Square, Canary Wharf, London E14 5DL Tel: 0171-293 2000/0171-345 2000 Fax: 0171-293 2435/0171-345 2435
Registered in England number 1908967 *Registered Office:* One Canada Square, Canary Wharf, London E14 5AP

HEART FELT PRODUCTIONS

Suites 139-140
Elm Park Mansion
Park Walk
London SW10 0AS

Tel: 0171 352 9689
Fax: 0171 376 8378

Geoffrey Perkins
Mr Comedy!
BBC Television
London W12

Directors:
Steve Oboto
Ainsley Parrott
Winston Obogo
Simone Durity
P. Amin

12th April 1998

Dear Geoffrey
<u>'CRAPPYFRUIT AND PINK KNICKERS!'</u>

Hi there! Gutted not to have heard from you re the above. This isn't a black thing, is it, Geoffrey? That the shit, my man – the brothers have taken over. Liz Reed was put in the clinic and the firm went pear-shaped. We moved in and picked up the pieces.

Anyway – here are two more concepts which might tighten your nuts.

1. 'I BLOW OFF IN PUBLIC BUT NEVER TAKE THE BLAME!'

Mad-cap Ginger Nut Chris Evans hosts a show in which celebs admit to rather anti-social habits!

2. 'WE GET TRAGEDIES BY THE TRUCK-LOAD!'

A game show based on 'The Price Is Right'. Folk in traction, wired up to kidney machines, on life support systems etc are wheeled on and contestants from the audience are invited to 'Come On Down!' and guess what compensation they got from the government. The winners get cash, off-the-road vehicles and holidays in Florida. There'll be something for the accident victims too.

Alternatively, the format could be closer to 'HAVE I GOT NEWS FOR YOU' or 'THEY THINK IT'S ALL OVER', with a wacky presenter (Mark Lamarr, Phill Jupitus) adjudicating between two teams or wise-cracking celebs. In this case, it would be the celebs who'd be guessing the compensation figures, while getting laughs from the victims' mishaps. Dad of four Leslie Harrison got £146,000 from Somerset Health Authority when a hospital stitched his testicles to his scrotum! Imagine the fun Lee Hurst, say, could have with that! (Press cutting enclosed).
Hey – give it up for the new players in town!
Peace, my man.

Winston Obogo.

Heart Felt Productions Limited

'A Tragedy Aired is a Tragedy Shared'

Linda Lord-Hogan
Harper Collins
77-85 Fulham Palace Road
London W6 8JB

Suites 139/140
Elm Park Mansions
Park Walk
LONDON
SW10 0AS

18th April 1998

Tel: 0171-352-9689
Fax: 0171-376-8378

Dear Linda,

Really great to get your letter of 11th March. It was a bit of a downer, natch, that Eddie Bell couldn't do 'SMILE PLEASE!'. but, hey, that's the way it goes. As you said: "Events did overtake us for a while."

I s'pose you were referring to the crap PR you got when those self-appointed academics criticised Rupert for dumping Chris Patten.

Not to worry, Linda! Dawn Airey, the sassy lassie who runs Channel 5, recently said: "Rupert Murdoch is my hero!" Confidentially, Linda, Dawn plans eventually to dump Channel 5 and move to Sky.

Speaking of which, she's just commissioned another development from us which might do it for Eddie. It's a two-parter entitled 'HOW TO TELL IF YOUR PARENTS AREN'T ON DRUGS'. We've retained volume rights and I now enclose alternative cover images by our Art Dept. You'll agree, I think, that no one on drugs would go out looking like this!

Plus, we're substantially progressing 'THE LITTLE BOOK OF REALLY BRILLIANT NEWS JUST WHEN YOU THOUGHT YOUR LIFE WAS DOWN THE FUCKING TOILET'. The idea is to cash in on 'The Little Book Of Calm' phenomena and I enclose examples on a separate sheet.

Over to you, Linda! I'm sure you'll persuade Eddie to come up with a two book deal!

Be good!

Yours,

Liz

Liz Reed.

Directors: Jeff Boyd Liz Reed Martin Jacques
Simon King, Angela Picano (Sicily)
Registered in England NO: 2905691

'HOW TO TELL IF YOUR PARENTS AREN'T ON DRUGS'

Projected Cover Design (1)

'HOW TO TELL IF YOUR PARENTS AREN'T ON DRUGS'

Projected Cover Design (2)

'THE LITTLE BOOK OF REALLY BRILLIANT NEWS
JUST WHEN YOU THOUGHT YOUR LIFE WAS
DOWN THE FUCKING TOILET'.

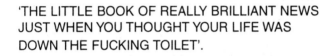

England 0 Cameroons 5

(Sheringham sent off)

A bus-load of comedians goes over a cliff. All saved.

PAGE 2

Except Mark Lamarr.

PAGE 3

And Phill Jupitus.

PAGE 4

In shocking case of mistaken identity, police arrest Richard Littlejohn for gross indecency in public lavatory. All charges dropped.

PAGE 5

But they gave him a good kicking anyway.

PAGE 6

On BBC1's 'Watchdog', Edward Enfield quizzes a common couple from Essex about their holiday in Spain. "Hullo Wayne and Sharon. Sorry about your holiday. Tell us what was wrong with it, would you?"

PAGE 7

"Nothing at all, you nosey old twat. It was brilliant."

PAGE 8

Lord Archer's P.A recently confused his medical records with his holiday arrangements. She cancelled his annual appointment at the Middlesex and booked him instead into the Royal Bath Hotel, Bournemouth.

PAGE 9

Whaddya reckon, Linda?

Impact soonest, yeah.

Liz

Liz

Where he underwent a prostate examination with a beach umbrella.

PAGE10

A Division o
Harper Collins *Pubishers*

7-85 Fulham Palace Road
Hammersmith
London W3 3JB

Telephone 0181-741 7070
Facsimile: 0181 307 4440

HarperCollins *Publishers*

14 May 1998

Liz Reed
Heart Felt Productions Ltd
Suites 139/140
Elm Park Mansions
LONDON SW10 0AS

Dear Liz,

Thanks for your letter of 12 May. I don't seem to recollect a letter of 18 April?

However, I have passed your draft onto the MD of our Trade Division for his perusal and either he or I will come back to you.

Kind regards.

Yours sincerely,

Linda Lord-Hogan
PA To Chairman

Registered as Harper Collins *Publishers* Ltd Scotland 1949 No: 273891, Westerhill Road, Bishopbriggs, Glasgow

HEART FELT PRODUCTIONS

Suites 139-140
Elm Park Mansion
Park Walk
London SW10 0AS

Directors:
Steve Oboto
Ainsley Parrott
Winston Obogo
Simone Durity
Aupade Buisson
Armit Singh

Tel: 0171 352 9689
Fax: 0171 376 8378

Paul Jackson
Head of Entertainment
The BBC
London W12

Dear Paul

Hey - what do you know? We've been pitching our concepts to the wrong guy at the BBC!

I'm talking about the 'CRAPPYFRUIT AND PINK KNICKERS!', 'I BLOW OFF IN PUBLIC BUT NEVER TAKE THE BLAME!' and 'WE GET TRAGEDIES BY THE TRUCKLOAD'

All pitched to Mr Comedy, Geoffrey Perkins (letters enclosed)!

Now Geoffrey tells us that these developments should have been pitched to you - Mr Entertainment!

Well,hey, if that's so that's fine with us, Paul, but we'd be obliged if you'd develop or reject as quickly as possible. We don't want you clogging up the creative pipeline for months like Geoffrey did.
So - impact with us soonest, yeah?
Peace my man

Winsln Obogo

Winston Obogo.

 **Production**

Controller of BBC Entertainment

8th May 1998

Winston Obogo
Heart Felt Productions Ltd
Suites 139/140 Elm Park Mansions
Park Walk
London
SW10 0AS

Dear Winston

Many thanks for letting me see your correspondence for three programme proposals. I am afraid none of them meet with our current scheduling needs and I am accordingly returning them to you.

Kind regards

Paul Jackson

Enc.

Heart Felt Productions Limited

'A Tragedy Aired is a Tragedy Shared'

Roxanne Vacca
The Roxanne Vacca Management
8 Silver Place
London W1R 3LJ

27th April 1998

Suites 139/140
Elm Park Mansions
Park Walk
LONDON
SW10 0AS
Tel: 0171-352-9689
Fax: 0171-376-8378

Dear Roxanne

I enclose a copy of a letter to Colin Jarvis at the BBC which I think is self-explanatory. Colin is the guy who tries to sell Brit formats to American TV. Basically we've been commissioned by Channel 4 to do a show on why the Yanks have no sense of irony. Colin has agreed to take part (copy of fax enclosed).

Okay, so we thought we had the perfect line-up until we saw 'Booked' a couple of weeks back, in which your client Arabella Weir (just <u>adore</u> her work) poked fun at the Yanks by reading extracts from the irony-free Book of Rules.

Hilarious or what, Roxanne!?!

I mean it was like, "Hey! There's a babe we gotta have on the show!" So - would she be free to appear in 'JUST WHAT <u>IS</u> IT WITH THE AMERICANS?', along with Colin Jarvis, Beryl Virtue, Marks and Gran, Zoe Ball, Joanna Lumley and Denise Van Outen?

We could film her at home or in your office - whichever suited her best. Just fax or mail me a suitable date (early June if possible) if Arabella is up for this in principle.

One other thing. Do you handle any other top comedy writers besides Arabella? I happen to know that the producers of 'The Larry Sanders Show' are unhappy with its lack of wide appeal in the UK and are keen to engage some English writers for the new season.
Do please mail your suggestions.
Hey - have a great one!
Yours,

Liz

Liz Reed.

Directors: Jeff Boyd Liz Reed Martin Jacques
Simon King, Angela Picano (Sicily)
Registered in England NO: 2905691

🗐001

Roxane Vacca

M A N A G E M E N T

Facsimile Cover Sheet

Attention: Liz Reed   Company: Heart Felt Productions Limited
To (Fax No.): 0171 376 8378   Date: 16th June 1998
From: Roxanne Vacca   Subject: Arabella Weir

Number of pages (including cover sheet): 1

Dear Liz Reed

Re: Just What Is It With The Americans – Arabella Weir

Further to your letter of 4th June I can confirm that Arabella will be available for
filming on Friday 26th June. The best times for her would be between 3pm and
6pm – would this work out for you?

Regards

Roxanne Vacca

A Division of
Harper Collins *Pubishers*

7-85 Fulham Palace Road
Hammersmith
London W3 3JB

Telephone 0181-741 7070
Facsimile: 0181 307 4440

HarperCollins *Publishers*

4 August, 1998

Liz Reed
Heart Felt Productions Ltd.
Elm Park Mansions
Park Walk
London SW10 0AS

Dear Ms Reed

HOW TO TELL IF YOUR PARENTS AREN'T ON DRUGS

Linda Lord-Hogan passed me the draft of HOW TO TELL IF YOUR PARENTS
AREN'T ON DRUGS. Apologies for the delay in getting back to you with a reply.

Several of us have read the draft here and whist we think it is an enjoyable read, we
do not feel that it fits comfortably into the shape of our list at this time.

This being so , I hope you will forgive me if I do not make the offer for the book
but wish you well for it elsewhere.

Very best wishes

Yours sincerely

Adrian Bourne
Managing Director - Trade Division

Registered as Harper Collins *Publishers* Ltd Scotland 1949 No: 273891, Westerhill Road, Bishopbriggs, Glasgow